A Man in Pain, A Life to Gain

# Cookfullnes

by Ian Taverner

*Coeliac Cooking For **All** Of The Family*

*Therapy, Power & Wellbeing*

London | New York

*Published by Clink Street Publishing 2020*



*First edition.*



*ISBN:*
*978-1-913568-79-5 - paperback*
*978-1-913568-80-1 - ebook*

# Dedications

I dedicate this book to my family, extended family, and especially my wonderful wife, and our beautiful girls, without whom I would literally not be standing.

I love you all so much xxxx

Also, to all of the amazing staff at the NHS Pain Specialist Hospital in Bath. You are truly remarkable people.

Finally, to the 'Pains in Bath' misfits, you know who you are (!), an unbreakable bond formed and unconditional love, support and humour XXX

We fight on!

# A Recipe For Success

In life you find some things that you like
If lucky, things that you love too
I don't mean marriage or things like that
More things that you like to do

Cooking has always been a passion of mine
Stoked years ago by my Ma
A wonderful cook she could make anything
And the fewest ingredients go far

Thankfully I never took after my Dad
Who could burn anything with ease
Famous for his signature dish
Of warm milk and cheese!

My creativity it did take a hit
When cooking became a chore
It hurts to even hold a spoon
So less definitely became more

But keeping your mind occupied
And trying all things new
Is such a good thing to try and do
Yes even a vindaloo!

The passion is back despite it all
And in this book you will see
Some recipes that I love to cook
That are fit for any family

# Cookfulness

***"a state of calm and warmth, awareness and enjoyment, readiness and nowness for before, during and after cooking"***

Cookfulness gives you the power to try it, use cooking as a therapy, Cookfulness IS wellbeing.

The art of making food people enjoy and, more importantly, you enjoy, is lost when suffering from chronic pain and mental health problems. Food is not just a fuel or sugary snacks when you are feeling low that pick you up and crash you down again.

***Create space for the Happy Stuff!!!***

There are many cooking and health books that are full of fantastic recipes and promises to improve your lifestyle, and some that are just plain naughty! However, in order to actually make any of these, you need to be able to cook and, more importantly, you need to have to want to cook!

When you are suffering from chronic pain conditions, such as fibromyalgia and arthritis etc., and mental health problems such as depression and anxiety etc., the last thing you want to do is open a cookbook and make wonder dishes. The brain and body will just say "NO!"

There are not many, if any, cookbooks that are focused on this first step, to actually want to cook in the first place.

Cookfulness is this very book!

## *Contemplation, preparation, exultation, revelation*

When you are in pain, be that physically and / or mentally, cooking is often the last thing on your mind.

Freezer food, bang it in the oven

Beige food, bang it in the oven

That's hard enough to do, I know!

Loving food is really hard, especially when you don't love yourself. Creativity though can spark your brain and body into life, giving you a purpose, a meaning for being. If you try practicing Cookfulness, using different guests, different dishes, it can really help you get your juices flowing and ignite the flames of cooking passion, ok, slowly at first.

Cooking has immense power, not just for you, but for family, friends, you name it. It's given me a role back, a reason, a purpose, a passion, a love, a desire, an excitement, a will, a real spark.

You are not just feeding people, you are nurturing, developing, preparing, sharing, communicating, loving, exciting, igniting, experimenting, socialising, revealing, inspiring, trying!!

# Cookfulness

Before you start to cook, even get yourself worked up about it, just take a second.......

**STOP, SIT, BREATHE.........**

**CLOSE YOUR EYES, BREATHE........**

**BREATHE, SLOW, BREATHE........**

Now visualise your family, your friends, people sat around a table enjoying **YOUR** food. They are talking, laughing, eating, smiling, just all very happy.

Keep seeing these happy faces, the look of deep satisfaction as they taste **YOUR** food. That pause as they take their first bite, the eyes closing and the "mmmmmm...." noises they make!!

Now, in your mind's eye you need to-

**Smell that food.........**

**Taste that food.........**

**See that food...........**

You **CAN** do this and **YOU WILL**.

Be proud of yourself, be strong and be present, here and now.

If you are having a bad day, I want to make it better.
If you are having a better day, I want to make it good.
If you are having a good day, I want to make it great.

If you are having a great day, good on you.

*Remember, less is more in good/great days*
and
*more is less in bad / better days*

This book is about helping you, who are suffering with chronic pain and/or depression, anxiety, panic, fatigue to want to and to be able to cook safely and productively no matter what type of day you are having.

It's full of useful hints and tips when you are struggling, through to when having a better day, no recipe is off limits.

Cookbooks often have lovely pictures of the dishes you are making, and how often are you so disappointed when yours looks nothing like it?! You then feel rubbish and want to give up. So, I have taken the bold decision to NOT show photos of the final dishes! Whatever you end up with WILL BE RIGHT! Be overjoyed with your results, be confident in your results and don't worry about what it should look like. It looks like it looks!

This book doesn't have fancy recipes with ingredients you need to travel miles to find. It doesn't consume you with days of preparation on end to even start it off. You don't need fancy gadgets or the help of a small army to make something!

I am coeliac, so no gluten or wheat, so the recipes here are aligned to that, but these recipes are for the entire family and more, they just happen to be gluten and wheat free too. If you aren't gluten free, and don't want to try it, then just replace anything specifically with your normal items.

I have the misfortune to be allergic to seafood as well! This does mean that, in this book, there are no specific recipes where seafood is the main or sub ingredient. I couldn't live with myself if I put in any recipes that I was not able to make and taste myself. I have though written where I believe seafood would add to or could be a replacement ingredient for a dish.

Remember, practice Cookfulness, keep those vivid happy pictures in your head. Use them whenever you are feeling low, tired or in pain, not just when cooking. Use those positive pictures and values to keep caring and remembering why you have a purpose, a passion, a desire, a reason, a power!

## About Me

I have always loved food, some say a little too much, and cooking and baking have been constant companions, memories of my mum and new memories with my girls. Losing the passion to cook was hard.

A cook book is something I have dreamt of for a good few years now, sometimes stronger than others, but never had the confidence, ability or stability to do it.

I have suffered from a long term chronic pain condition, fibromyalgia, for the last 10 years or so and have recently also had to have both my hips replaced due to arthritis. A series of horrendous events also led to my mental health declining rapidly, with depression and anxiety enveloping me.

The two together erupted like an angry volcano, leaving me at times unable to walk, function, think, talk, not much at all!

Apart from my family, cooking and music were my real passions in life. Due to chronic pain, I lost the last two and almost the first.

How deeply and darkly chronic pain can affect you and those around you can never be underestimated. Losing sight of what really matters and what makes you get up in the morning is the first thing to go and the hardest to get back. Some very wise people told me recently that you can't change your thoughts, feelings, emotions, but you can change your actions and what you do about it.

Easier said than done, oh yes!

However, if you can ignite the fires of what makes (made) you tick, be it family, friends, lovers, food, exercise, whatever, then you are one step along the path, the right path.

Cooking has the power to make people smile, make them drool, make them excited. That's just those eating it!

Cooking can be great for your mental and physical health, whether ill or not. For me, it's given me back a reason, a target, a love of life. How powerful is that!

Cooking can though be absolutely horrendous for people like me, in pain physically and mentally. Anxiety, fear, panic, pain, brain fog can all make it extremely hard to get out of bed, let alone cook.

It is a painful reality that myself with both physical and mental pain combinations created 3 roles for my wife. Firstly a mum to our girls, secondly a carer for me and thirdly a dad to our girls. Everything.

What better motivation than trying to correct that!

I am now sticking my (sore) neck out and starting to move forwards. I found a light, not just at the end of the tunnel, but illuminating the whole thing! You will see from my dedications of this book, that there is a team of people at the NHS Pain Specialist Centre in Bath that I / we owe a huge debt of gratitude to. Their patience, commitment and sheer excellence has given me a new chance of life, one I thought was just not possible a few short months ago. Am I still in horrific pain? YES! But, they have helped me find ways to cope that little bit better with the pain and torment and increase both mine and my family's quality of life.

I had lost my love of cooking, of music, of everything, but now am finding that spark again. With that spark has also come an amazing creative surprise, with poetry flying out at hyper speed!

I have included just a few of them in this book as they are both relevant to the food and to the battle we have each day just to get through, to try and have a life at all.

I am here to show you that there is a way. It isn't always obvious, most often isn't, but please, please keep persevering and believe there is a way for you to move forwards. Try this book, just give a few recipes a go, listen to some music, practice some **Cookfulness** and enjoy!

# Hints & Tips

These can apply to anyone but in particular are aimed at people like me who suffer on a daily basis with mind and body.

Cooking can be adapted to make things easier on a bad day, or test you a bit on a great one, but with the same results.

My first, and really biggest and best tip is-

**Things can and will go wrong!!**

It's ok, just treat it as a bit of a laugh, step back, re-cookfulness yourself, and try again. Don't panic.

## Physical pain

If your hands aren't working well and chopping feels a push too far, **always have frozen in your kit bag**

Frozen is often as good as, if not better than fresh as it is usually quick frozen and doesn't just apply to peas and sweetcorn! There are some absolute essentials I always have in the freezer ready for those rough days:

- **Frozen chopped mixed peppers** - stir fries, Ragu, you name it
- **Frozen chopped garlic** - the base for so many dishes
- **Frozen chopped ginger** - same as above
- **Frozen chopped chilli** - same as above
- **Frozen chorizo** - adds bit of spice to everything
- **Frozen bacon** - smoked is especially good
- **Frozen chopped onion (white and red)** - never be without this - starts loads and loads of dishes!
- **Frozen spinach** - great to add to curries
- **Frozen chopped herbs** - all you need, stay fresh and don't live at the back of your cupboard lurking for years!
- **Frozen mixed beans** - chilli's, soups, you name it
- **Frozen fruit**- smoothies, desserts

Not just for when you are not great, use them all of the time. Also it will save you a lot of money and cuts down on waste - winner!

## Brain Fog

Simplicity is what you need! Batch cook on better / good days and keep in re-useable containers in the portion sizes you need and in the freezer. They are there for you when your brain hurts. It's still homemade, by you and still delicious!

## Anxiety & Pain

- I've marked the really key stages of each recipe with a KEY, so you can see them ahead, and the really really important are in bold too!
- The step guides are there to take you easily through each recipe.
- In pretty much every cook book, recipes will have a 'preparation time' and a 'cooks for' time, all very useful and I've got them in here too! However, these timings are only for when you are having a good or great day and can do everything at a reasonable speed and to a reasonable level of skill. So, I have invented **'Give Yourself Time'** ! This sits alongside the other 2 and is the time it's likely to take you when having a bad or better day, so giving you the time and space to plan ahead and not get into a panic later on.
- Try where you can to work backwards from the timings you've been given, so you know when to start and to give yourself sufficient time to finish. Then, add a bit more time on!
- For most recipes, pre-heating the oven is step 1, so try not to forget as it can set you back a long time waiting for it to heat up otherwise.
- Buy yourself a little timer, they are like gold dust! You don't then have to try and remember half way through what time you put things in, how long is left etc.! You can get really cheap ones and that's all you need! Most phones now have timers on them, so use it!
- I've set out at the top of each recipe, exactly what pans, pots, utensils etc. you will need. This again is different and designed to let you get everything prepared up front, making sure you've got what you need or can get hold of it, rather than finding out mid cook!
- Widen the kitchen! Just because you are cooking doesn't mean you have to stay in the kitchen. Use what help you have at home, for instance, when use

walking aids like me, chopping and balancing can be tricky and dangerous! So use your dining table and sit at a chair, it's much safer and easier. Or, if you have a good TV tray (shame on you!!), use this whilst sat. Also, use your family, they will almost certainly have the ability to help if you need it so don't be afraid to ask. Get them involved and help make your life easier.

## More Hints & Tips

### Gluten & Wheat Free Food

- Not all gluten free food is wheat free and not all wheat free food is coeliac. Always check and double check ingredients.
- Coeliac food and availability has come an awful long way in recent years, which is great. BUT, still in most supermarkets and stores, the 'Free From' sections are hidden away at the back and you feel like you've been targeted as 'one of those'! Also, they make you walk the furthest to get there! Free from areas are great, but often it's the sugary sweet stuff, there's not a great range and it's very expensive. Some things you do need to get there, like pasta, bread etc., but often there are most other things in the general store, it's just a matter of finding them. I promise you, you will save a lot of money!

For example, a jar of specialty gluten free pasta sauce can cost £2.99 in some stores, but their own brand pasta sauce, same size but not advertised as gluten and wheat free, but naturally is, costs a pound or more less! You will be surprised how much is possible!

**Internet Vs Actual Shopping -** going out shopping can be incredibly intimidating, scary and anxious, invariably bringing pain on too. So internet shopping seems an absolute godsend! And it is .......but, with internet shopping you are likely ordering the same things over and over again, and never leaving your home. Don't kid yourself that chatting to the shopping delivery driver is a social life! I've been there and done it, so I know you know what I mean!
Try physically going to a shop. Start small, just a few things to get and then

home. Try gradually reducing the amount of internet shopping and supplementing with real face to face shopping.

Believe me, there is nothing better for the soul than seeing, smelling, touching different foods, checking for ripeness, wondering what you would do with things. And seeing something and thinking "what the heck is that?" That's what you should buy and experiment with!
The temptation, no the urge, will be to get out of there. Don't! Go as slowly as you can, then go even slower! You will feel daft to start with but the slow pace lets you take everything in, calms you down, gives you confidence, go on, try it!

When you get to your usual potatoes, look at what others there are, the different types and what you could use them for. A salad, a mash, a roast, a chip, try something different.

**Gadgets, Pans & Utensils** - if you are like me you will love these. See them on TV or in a mag, think, "ooo, I like that", then *you know who* delivers it to your door the very next day. Have you used it yet??? We've all got a redundant spiralizer sat at the back of the cupboard haven't we!? You really don't need that much to be able to cook really well. My main items are:

- A good knife - just one good sharp one
- A chopping board
- A wok, or like me, a large frying pan that has curved sides, like a squashed wok!
- A couple of good sized sauce pans and lids
- A wooden spoon
- A large plastic spoon
- A pair of tongues or grabbers
- A plastic spatula
- A mixing bowl
- A timer
- A set of weighing scales
- An electric blitzer
- A meat thermometer - just cheap and basic
- A measuring jug
- A casserole dish and lid

**The Tweak!** - virtually every recipe can be changed almost beyond recognition by adding one or two extra ingredients. This makes cooking both exciting and a lot easier because you can take a basic recipe, like mine in here for a Bolognese, and make many, many more dishes from it as the base. No-one needs to know how easy it was, do they?!

My store cupboard absolute musts for the tweak are:

- Curry powder - various strengths and colours and instantly takes you to the sub continental
- Chinese 5 spice - say no more
- Ginger - frozen, chopped or fresh grated adds a twang of heat
- Cinnamon - for savory dishes it adds a Middle Eastern twist.
- Cardamom seeds - to rice or dishes adds savory authenticity
- Turmeric - great for you, turns everything orange and really tasty
- Asafoetida - weird one but, trust me, added to any vegetable dish it transforms it!
- Mixed spice - wonderful festive flavours for sweet things
- Italian mixed herbs - just lift you to Turin and Rome
- Paprika / smoked paprika - spice and smoke
- Gluten free Worcester sauce - great with mince dishes
- Gluten free soy sauce - instantly lifts rice and noodle dishes

**Growing your own** - sounds a pain but it really is great fun. Start small! To say to someone, this dish has my own home grown produce in it is so amazing. Herbs are a really good start, indoors or outdoors. Ones you will use the most are:

- Basil - for salads, tomato sauces, pizzas etc.
- Coriander - for salads, Asian and Indian food
- Mint - for salads, potatoes and desserts

Nurturing and growing something, looking after it, using it in your own dishes, is just great. Get the family involved if you can and create togetherness and excitement.

If you get the bug, maybe try some potatoes in grow bags, carrots, onions, salad leaves maybe. Not everything ever works each time, but that's part of the fun! It extends your sense of purpose, your ability to be busy and productive. It's incredibly addictive, I promise you!

**Music** - they say that music is the food of love! Well I say food is the music of love too!!

Music is so important to set you up.

Create your own Cookfulness playlists.

If you are like me, cooking in the weekdays is different to weekends. You have less time to prepare, cook and eat, with busy family lives, whereas weekends you can take your time over Sunday lunch for instance.

Tailor your Cookfulness playlists accordingly, the loud and fast music for weekdays, to get you going, and the longer playlists for weekends. Have fun with it and use it as part of your Cookfulness experience.

Play your absolute favourites as loud as you are allowed, sing like there's no tomorrow, dance a bit (if you can!).

For me it is the '80s!! My teenage years and music that just sets me going every time!

Please, please, please try and avoid the temptation to pick out tunes that are painfully slow or have dark memories attached to them. It is easy to do, but go for the ones that have great memories attached, you dancing away with your mates, giving it large!

Use more recent memories, a great movie soundtrack, someone you just saw on TV and loved the song. Try getting some albums, not just shuffle play, and find some music you had never heard before, it's great!

Cooking is all about enjoyment, so enjoy it, and make it a real experience each and every time!!

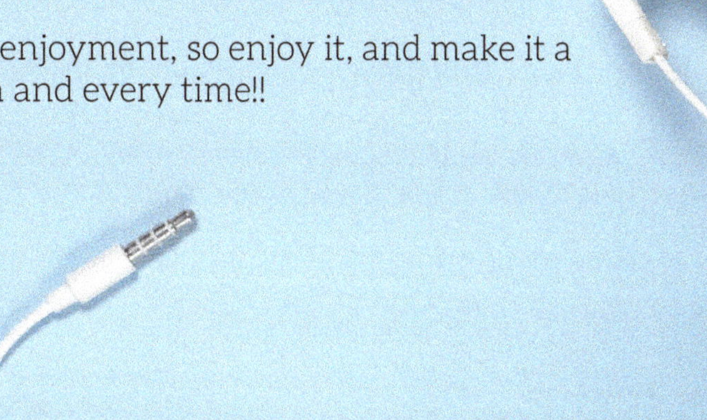

# *Spaghetti Head*

I likened my brain to a plate of spaghetti
So tangled and messed up inside
No way to determine what was what
No person to act as a guide

I love spaghetti, so why is it bad
My head going this way and that
The only thing I can think to do
Is put on another hat

The hats they are things to hide the real me
Put on to protect and disguise
But a messed-up head can always be seen
Just by the look in my eyes

So how to untangle the mess it is
Takes courage and desire
Someone to help you dig in the right places
Will surely stoke the fires

But don't be afraid, keep on looking
And answers they will start to appear
A plate full of a pile of spaghetti
Is really nothing to fear

Slowly, slowly the spaghetti straightens
Into lines not twists and turns
From end to end you can now see
But still your stomach churns

Then the clouds they part and everything's clear
A chance to take stock and think
Now all the spaghetti is one by one
Sit back, breathe and blink!

# Index

## Early & Late



## Anytime



## For Me and / or Family

## The Sweet Stuff

## Party Time



## Handies

# Early & Late

# Smoothies

*A great morning start or anytime boost of goodness*

*All of these start with the same base, then add the different tastes and colours! Remember you eat with your eyes too so multi-colour experiences are as good as anything for you*

**Difficult rating::** ★☆☆☆☆
**Serves:** 2-6
**Cooking time:** 0 mins
**Preparation time:** 5 mins
**Give Yourself Time:** 10 mins

**You Will Need**

*Blender / blitzer*
*Measuring jug*
*Knife*
*Weighing scales*
*Chopping board*
*Metal spoon*

## Basic Smoothie

**Ingredients**

- ½ banana (ripe) peeled and sliced
- 150g natural yoghurt (plain)
- 150ml water
- 100ml orange juice (no bits and unsweetened)

**Method**

*Put all of the ingredients into the blender*
*Whizz until the consistency you want, smooth obviously best!*
*Pour and serve!*

# The Green One

*You'll feel great!*

**Difficult rating:** ★☆☆☆☆
**Serves:** 2-6
**Cooking time:** 0 mins
**Preparation time:** 5 mins
**Give Yourself Time:** 10 mins

**You Will Need**

*As per basic one*

## Ingredients

- Same as basic one, plus
- Handful of fresh spinach (frozen also great but use a little less)
- Handful of kale (as above)
- 100ml water
- 2 ice cubes (reduce to 1 if using frozen spinach)
- 1 × ripe avocado peeled, stoned and chopped
- Another ½ banana peeled and chopped
- (optional) sprinkle of mixed powdered super seeds (linseed, chia, flax etc)

## Method

*Add to the base mix and blitz to smooth*
*If you have too much, do in a couple of batches*
*Pour and serve!*

# The Red One

*Makes you smile!*

**Difficult rating:** ★☆☆☆☆
**Serves:** 2-6
**Cooking time:** 0 mins
**Preparation time:** 5 mins
**Give Yourself Time:** 10 mins

**You Will Need**

*As per basic one*

## Ingredients

- Same as basic one, plus
- 150g fresh or frozen strawberries
- 150g fresh or frozen raspberries
- (optional) sprinkle of supersedes (linseed, chia, flax etc)

## Method

*Add to the base mix and blitz to smooth*
*If you have too much, do in a couple of batches*
*Pour and serve!*

# The Purple One

*Deep & meaningful!*

**Difficult rating:** ★☆☆☆☆
**Serves:** 2-6
**Cooking time: 0mins**
**Preparation time: 5mins**
**Give Yourself Time: 10mins**

**You Will Need**

*As per basic one*

## Ingredients

- Same as basic one, plus
- 250g mixed frozen berries (black, blue and raspberries)
- (optional) sprinkle of supersedes (linseed, chia, flax etc)

## Method

*Add to the base mix and blitz to smooth*
*If you have too much, do in a couple of batches*
*Pour and serve!*

# The Yellow One

*Truly tropical!*

**Difficult rating:** ★☆☆☆☆
**Serves:** 2-6
**Cooking time:** 0mins
**Preparation time:** 5mins
**Give Yourself Time:** 10mins

## You Will Need

*As per basic one*

## Ingredients

- Same as basic one, plus
- 250g mixed frozen tropical fruit (mango, papaya, pineapple, melon)
- (optional) sprinkle of supersedes (linseed, chia, flax etc)

## Method

*Add to the base mix and blitz to smooth*
*If you have too much, do in a couple of batches*

*Pour and serve!*

### Smoothie Hints & Tips 

Really experiment!!

It's great fun and you really can't go wrong

You may stumble on your own fantastic smoothie mix!

If it is getting too thick just add more water or orange juice

### Ways To Change 

Try adding:

Grated ginger (frozen also good) for a real kick

Chilli flakes (or frozen chilli) for that hot and cold spice

Mint – fresh or frozen for a fragrant tang

Lime / lemon juice and zest to get the taste buds firing

Cinnamon for a fragrant whack

# Burcher

*Makes at least a weeks' worth!*

**Difficult rating:** ★☆☆☆☆
**Serves:** A week for one
**Cooking time:** 10 mins
**Preparation time:** 5 mins
**Give Yourself Time:** 25 mins

**You Will Need**

*Baking tray*
*Large mixing bowl*
*Chopping Board*
*Airtight storage jar or Tupperware*
*Blender / blitzer or mini spice blender (freezer bag and rolling pin if not)*
*Knife*
*Metal mixing spoon*

### Ingredients

- 1 × bag gluten free oats / porridge oats
- 2 × large handfuls of mixed dried fruit (cranberries, raisins, sultanas)*
- 1 × large handful of mixed nuts (your choice but walnuts, cashews, pistachios are good)*
- Scattering of mixed powdered super seeds (chia, linseed, flax etc)*
- 2 × handfuls of larger dried fruit roughly chopped (fig, apricot etc)*

**These all come in made up packet form from most supermarkets and stores so you don't have to do it yourself!*

### Method

KEY – pre-heat the oven to 200C

Empty the bag of oats onto the baking tray and spread evenly

Blitz the nuts to small pieces (if no blitzer use a freezer bag, slightly open, and bash with a rolling pin)

Scatter the nuts over the oats

Scatter the mixed super seeds over the oat mix too and combine all to well mixed

KEY TIMER – put the tray into the oven for 10 mins

Bring out and allow to cool in the tray

Tip into a large bowl

Add the mixed dried fruit, large and small, and mix well with a metal spoon

Carefully add to your storage jar(s) and use when want

### Hints & Tips

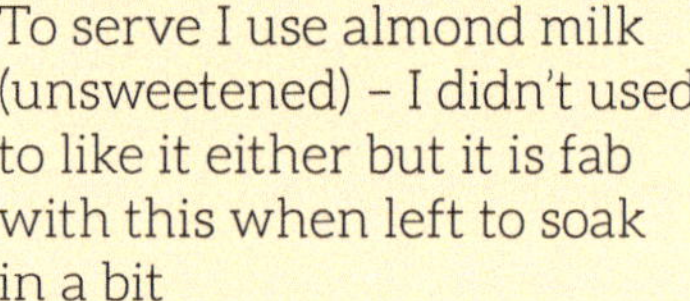

To serve I use almond milk (unsweetened) – I didn't used to like it either but it is fab with this when left to soak in a bit

You can use milk also or your favourite yoghurt

### Ways To Change

Use different dried fruits

Use different nut mixes

Use different super seeds

Make different flavours and see what you like best – keep experimenting though to keep it exciting!

# Overnight Oats

*Yum!*
*Just need to remember to do the night before!*

**Difficult rating:** ★☆☆☆☆
**Serves:** 1
**Cooking time:** 0 mins
**Preparation time:** 5 mins
**Give Yourself Time:** 10 mins

**You Will Need**

*Mixing bowl*
*Teaspoon & Tablespoon*
*Wooden spoon*
*Measuring jug*
*Bowl or jar to serve*
*Measuring scales*

**Ingredients**

- 50g gluten free porridge oats
- Pinch salt
- ¼ tspn ground cinnamon
- 2 tbspns plain natural yogurt
- 100ml almond milk or your choice of milk

**Method**

In a bowl mix the porridge oats, cinnamon, milk and salt and leave overnight in the fridge

When ready to eat, put the porridge mix into the base of a serving bowl and top with the yoghurt

*If the mix is very stiff add a little more milk*

# Fruit Layered Overnight Oats

*Yummier!*
*Still need to remember to do the night before!*

**Difficult rating:** ★☆☆☆☆
**Serves:** 1
**Cooking time:** 0 mins
**Preparation time:** 5 mins
**Give Yourself Time:** 10 mins

**You Will Need**

*Mixing bowl*
*Teaspoon & Tablespoon*
*Wooden spoon*
*Measuring jug*
*Bowl or jar to serve*
*Measuring scales*

**Ingredients**

- Same as overnight oats plus
- 50g mixed berries (frozen is best here)
- 1 tbspn honey

**Method**

The night before, take half the porridge mix and put into a serving bowl or jar

Top with half the frozen mixed berries and a drizzle of honey

Add the remainder of the oat mix

Top with the remaining mixed berries and honey

Put into the fridge overnight

Top with yoghurt when ready to eat

# Tropical Layered Overnight Oats

*Yummier!*
*Still need to remember to do the night before!*

**Difficult rating:** ★☆☆☆☆
**Serves:** 1
**Cooking time:** 0 mins
**Preparation time:** 5 mins
**Give Yourself Time:** 10 mins

### You Will Need

*Mixing bowl*
*Teaspoon & Tablespoon*
*Wooden spoon*
*Measuring jug*
*Bowl or jar to serve*
*Measuring scales*

### Ingredients

- Same as overnight oats plus
- 50g mixed tropical fruit (frozen is best here)
- 1 tbspn honey

### Method

The night before, take half the porridge mix and put into a serving bowl or jar

Top with half the frozen mixed tropical fruit and a drizzle of honey

Add the remainder of the oat mix

Top with the remaining mixed tropical fruit and honey

Put into the fridge overnight

Top with yoghurt when ready to eat

### Hints & Tips

Use different frozen fruit to mix it up

Try scattering dried mixed superseeds onto the yoghurt topping

Add a sprinkle of mixed chopped nuts to the top of the yoghurt

A splosh of maple syrup on top of the yoghurt adds some lovely sweetness

Sprinkle some caster sugar onto the mixed frozen berries if you aren't a fan of maple syrup or honey

# Eggs!

*Wonderful, versatile, any time of the day!*

*Eggs can be amazing or leave you stumped and frustrated with either dry egg bullets or sloppy under cooked whites*

*These are simple and easy ways to get it right all of the time – honestly!*

## Poached Eggs

*No vinegar & no swirling!*

**Difficult rating:** ★★½☆☆
**Serves:** as many as you make
**Cooking time:** 5 mins
**Preparation time:** 3-4 mins
**Give Yourself Time:** 15 mins

**You Will Need**

*Deep frying pan*
*Cup*
*Large metal spoon with slots in (but don't worry if not)*

### Ingredients

- **FRESH** Free-range eggs as many as you are needing
- Salt and pepper
- 1 × cup
- Kitchen paper to dry eggs

### Method

Heat about 4 inches of water in the pan to just simmering – NOT boiling **KEY**

Put a pinch of salt into the water

Crack an egg into the cup

KEY TIMER – gently pour the egg from the cup into the water and repeat for as many eggs as you need

**Set timer for 3mins for first one in**

The white should be just set and the yolk has a wobble

Remove with a slotted metal spoon and pat dry top and bottom

Sprinkle salt and pepper on top and serve as you want, on gluten free toast, bagels or pitta etc

### Hints & Tips 

**Fresh eggs are MUCH** better for poaching as the whites don't spread or are watery

**Eggs at room temperature** are better all round

If doing multiple eggs, to ensure you know which one went in, I put the first one where the handle is and then go clockwise around the pan

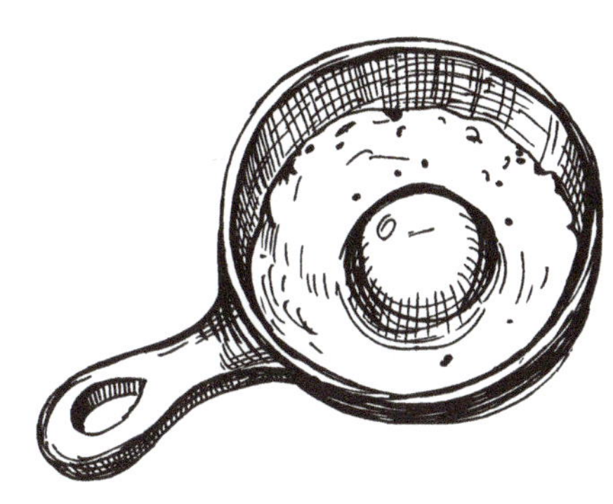

# Boiled Eggs

*Classic & Lovely*

**Difficult rating:** ★☆☆☆☆
**Serves:** as many as you make
**Cooking time:** 6-10 mins
**Preparation time:** 5 mins
**Give Yourself Time:** 20 mins

## You Will Need

*Small saucepan*
*Metal spoon*

## Ingredients

- **FRESH** Free-range eggs as many as you are needing
- Salt and pepper

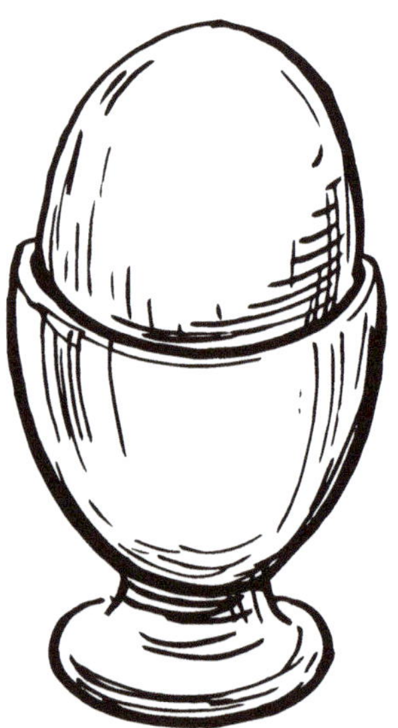

## Method

Fill the saucepan with water about 2/3rds of the way up and bring to the boil

KEY – make sure it is a low rolling boil and not boiling over

Using the metal spoon, carefully place the eggs into the boiling water, making sure they don't drop in hard and crack on the bottom or sides

KEY TIMER – depending on how you want your eggs, set the timer for:

6 mins for soft boiled eggs

8 mins for salad ready eggs

10 mins for hard boiled eggs

Remove the eggs with the spoon when your time is up and serve how you wish

# Scrambled Eggs

*A meal for any time of the day!*

**Difficult rating:** ★★★☆☆
**Serves:** as many as you make
**Cooking time:** 3-5 mins
**Preparation time:** 10 mins
**Give Yourself Time:** 20 mins

### You Will Need

*Small saucepan (larger if doing a lot at once)*
*Rubber / plastic spatula*
*Whisk or fork*
*Bowl/jug for mixing*

### Ingredients

- **FRESH** Free-range eggs – allow 2 per person
- Salt and pepper
- Knob of butter

### Hints & Tips

**Eggs at room temperature** are better all round

Try adding some chopped chives to the eggs right at the end for a lovely oniony hit

Adding some bacon bits gives a lovely crunch too

### Method

Break the eggs into the bowl or jug and whisk until well combined

Add a pinch of salt and pepper

KEY – melt the butter in the saucepan over a **low heat** – you don't want bubbling or fizzing butter here

When melted, pour in the eggs and immediately start stirring with the spatula

KEY - Keep stirring and going around the sides of the pan to free any large lumps and remove any sticking to the bottom

It is up to you how you like your eggs, either well-cooked and firm or runnier and liquidy.

KEY – eggs continue to cook even when they are off the heat so get them to just a bit looser of a texture than you want finally and take them off then. Practice and experience will help you get this point just right so don't worry if it is a bit hit and miss to start with!

# Eggy Bread

*Always a winner and a great way to use up old bread!*

**Difficult rating:** ★★☆☆☆
**Serves:** 2-4
**Cooking time:** 5 mins
**Preparation time:** 15 mins
**Give Yourself Time:** 25 mins

**You Will Need**

*Large deep frying pan*
*Spatula*
*Whisk or fork*
*Large mixing bowl*
*Large plate*

## Ingredients

- 3 free range eggs
- 4 pieces gluten free white bread (closer to stale is better here!)
- Pinch salt
- Pinch of cinnamon or mixed spice (optional)
- Knob of butter per bread piece
- Splash of milk

## Method

KEY – preheat the oven to 160C for keeping the breads warm

Break the eggs into the bowl and whisk until smooth

Add a pinch of salt, a splash of milk, the cinnamon or mixed spice (optional the spices here) and combine with the whisk

KEY – add a knob of butter to the frying pan and cook until starts to bubble

If you can get a whole piece of bread directly into the egg mixture in the bowl, dunk it in so it is covered in the mixture but don't leave it too long or it will get soggy and break

If the bowl is too small, pour some of the mixture onto the plate and lay the bread in it one side, then turns it to cover the other, again being quick so it doesn't go soggy

Shake off any excess egg mixture and add the bread to the frying pan on one side

KEY – leave the bread untouched for a minute, don't shake it or turn it, just let it sit in the hot butter

Using the spatula or tongues, check when the first side goes golden brown, then turn it over and repeat for the other side

When done, remove and add to a plate and put into the oven to keep warm whilst you do the remaining eggy breads

### Hints & Tips

You can serve this eggy bread as part of a good old fashioned cooked English breakfast, or

You can serve it as a sweet dish with a dusting of icing sugar and some ice cream, or

Just have it on its own, magic!

### Ways To Change

Add your favourite sweet spices to the egg mix

# Yoghurt Toppings

*Pimp up yoghurt to make it more interesting for breakfast!*

**Difficult rating:** ★☆☆☆☆
**Serves:** As many as want to
**Cooking time:** 0 mins
**Preparation time:** 5 mins
**Give Yourself Time:** 10 mins

## You Will Need

*Knife*
*Metal spoon*
*Chopping board*
*Serving bowls*

## Ingredients

Yoghurt of your choice, from

- Natural
- Greek
- Flavoured
- Skir – plain or flavoured

Choose from:

- Honey
- Handful of chopped mixed nuts – crushed or blitzed
- Frozen fruits (put in fridge night before)
- Maple syrup
- Any leftover smoothies you have
- Any Burcher left to spare
- Super seed powder mix (chia, linseed etc)

## Hints & Tips

Don't hold back!

## Ways To Change

Mix it up, change it every day, try different combinations and flavours

Try adding some fresh fruit as well

Add some herbs like mint for an added twist

## Method

Imagine you are on holiday in a beautiful resort...............

You arrive at the buffet breakfast, get some yoghurt in a bowl and then......

Go for it!

# Anytime

# Pancakes

*A family favourite and not just for pancake day!*
*Great to do with the kids*

**Difficult rating:** ★☆☆☆☆
**Serves:** 4
**Cooking time:** 10 mins
**Preparation time:** 25 mins
**Give Yourself Time:** 40 mins

**You Will Need**

*Measuring jug*
*Spatula*
*Weighing scales*
*Whisk*
*Frying pan*
*Mixing bowl*
*Deep metal spoon*

## Ingredients

- 125g Gluten Free Plain Flour
- 1 egg (free range if can)
- 250ml milk (your choice but semi-to-full better)
- 1 knob butter
- Rapeseed oil or spray

## Method

KEY - preheat oven to 160C to keep pancakes warm

Sift the flour into a large bowl

Make a well in the centre of the flour with your hands or a spoon

Crack the egg directly into the well

Pour in a quarter of the milk

Whisk thoroughly with a metal whisk

KEY **- Once you have a smooth paste with no lumps add another quarter of the milk and whisk again**

When a smooth paste, add the rest of the milk and give a final whisk

KEY **- Leave to rest for 20mins if you can**

Whisk again before using

Spray some oil or pour a tablespoon of oil into a shallow frying pan

Heat to a medium heat

Put in a ladle full of mixture, or enough to just fill the pan base

Once the sides come away from the pan and you can see it is golden brown underneath, flip (or just turn if not feeling brave!)

Once gold on both sides, remove and set aside on some kitchen paper, keeping warm in the oven until you have all of the pancakes ready

### Hints & Tips

Try to leave the pancake mix for at least 20 mins once first mixed, to rest

If you pour the mix from a bowl into a large jug, you can pour directly into the pan for more control

If you are feeling really bad, get the kids to help or even do this with you just there. It's great to encourage them to cook and for family strength.

### Ways To Change

Add sugar and lemon juice for a traditional pancake

Tray adding your favourite chocolate spread for some decadence!

Add some of your favourite soft fruits (strawberries, raspberries, blueberries etc.) a bit of natural yoghurt and roll it up

# So Tasty Breakfast Cereal Bars

*So much better and cheaper than buying them!*
*Energy lasts longer, no crash and dash!*

**Difficult rating:** ★★☆☆☆
**Makes:** 16
**Cooking time:** 25-30 mins
**Preparation time:** 10 mins
**Give Yourself Time:** 50 mins

### You Will Need

*Measuring jug*
*Spatula*
*Weighing scales*
*Whisk*
*Knife*
*Large Mixing bowl*
*Chopping Board*
*Airtight storage container*
*Baking tray*
*Tablespoon*

### Ingredients

- 100g soft butter (room temp)
- 50g dried cranberries
- 25g light muscovado sugar
- 75g sultanas
- 2 tbspns golden syrup
- 25g sunflower seeds
- 125g gluten free millet or corn flakes
- 25g linseeds
- 50g quinoa
- 40g unsweetened desiccated coconut
- 2 eggs slightly beaten (free range if can)

### Hints & Tips

These will **keep for a good week** in an airtight container.........that's if you haven't eaten them all by then!

Using room temp butter makes it a whole load easier to start

### Ways To Change

Add in your own combinations of nuts, seeds and fruits

Chia seeds are good, as are flax

### Method

KEY - Preheat the oven to 180c fan

Grease a 28 × 20 cm shallow rectangular baking tin

Beat together the butter, sugar and syrup until creamy

Add all of the remaining ingredients and beat well until combined

Turn into the tin and level the surface with the back of a spoon

KEY – **TIMER** Bake for 25-30 mins until golden brown

Leave to cool in the tin

When cold, turn onto a wooden board and carefully cut into 16 portions using a serrated knife

Store in an air tight container

# Potato Drop Scones

*So versatile can be used in any part of the day*

**Difficult rating:** ★☆☆☆☆
**Serves:** 4
**Cooking time:** 10 mins
**Preparation time:** 20 mins
**Give Yourself Time:** 35 mins

## You Will Need

*Measuring jug*
*Spatula*
*Weighing scales*
*Whisk*
*Frying pan*
*Mixing bowl*
*Knife*
*Chopping board*
*Teaspoon*
*Potato masher*

## Ingredients

- 550g large potatoes (maris piper best)
- Rapeseed oil for frying
- 1 & ½ tspns gluten free baking powder
- 2 medium eggs (free range best)
- 75ml milk (your choice but semi to full best)
- Salt and pepper

## Method

Peel and cut the potatoes into small chunks (same size as best can for even cooking)

KEY – **TIMER** Cook the potatoes in a large pan of boiling water (lightly salted), for **15 mins or until completely tender**

Drain the potatoes well, let them dry and then return to the pan and mash, until as smooth as can get

Leave to cool further

Beat the baking powder into the potatoes

Then add the eggs, milk, salt and pepper to taste, and beat until smooth

Once everything is combined, heat a tablespoon of oil in a frying pan

Drop heaped dessert spoons of the mixture into the pan, spacing slightly apart

Fry for 3-4 minutes each side, turning when golden brown

Once brown on both sides, keep warm on a plate until all the drop scones are ready

## Hints & Tips

KEY - It is **better to overcook** the potatoes than undercook when boiling as easier to mash

Great on their own for breakfast or brunch

You can keep some of the un-fried mixture in the fridge for the following day if you want to – making ahead for later in the day is also worth it if not

## Ways To Change

Add some spring onion (scallion to my wife) for an Irish twist

Add some curry powder for an Indian twist

For the really filthy of you, put a large one between buttered bread for an amazing sandwich!

# No Bake Tiffin Tray

*No Cooking required here!*

**Difficult rating:** ★★½☆☆
**Serves:** A Lot!
**Cooking time:** 0 mins
**Preparation time:** 20 mins
**Give Yourself Time:** 30 mins *(plus 1-1 ½ hours in fridge to set)*

**You Will Need**

*8 inch square cake tin*
*Grease proof paper*
*Scissors*
*Sauce pan*
*Weighing scales*
*Spatula*
*Teaspoon*
*Knife*
*Chopping board*

## Ingredients

- 300g gluten free digestive biscuits – crushed
- 150g dried mixed fruits (cranberries, sultanas etc)
- 250g gluten free dark chocolate broken into pieces (70% cocoa min)
- 150g butter
- 150g soft brown sugar
- 1 tspn mixed spice

## Method

Cut the grease proof paper so it will fit into the bottom of the cake tin and also up the sides about half way up (it doesn't need to be neat!)

KEY - In the saucepan, add the dark chocolate, sugar and butter and **gently melt it – do not boil it!**

Once combined and all melted, take it off the heat

Stir in the crushed digestive biscuits, mixed fruit and mixed spice to combine well

Spoon the mixture into the lined cake tin, pushing it into the corners and getting as even as you can

Put it into the fridge to set – takes min 1 hour

Take it out of the fridge, pull out of the tin using the grease proof paper and onto a chopping board

Cut into pieces of the size of your choice and enjoy!

**Hints & Tips**

Be gentle with the chocolate mix when melting, take your time!

**Ways To Change**

Try using different gluten free biscuits – so ginger or cookies etc

Use different dried mixed fruits

Add a pinch of salt and a pinch of chilli flakes for a kick

For the adults only, a drop of run or brandy in the chocolate, butter mix gives it a whole new meaning!

You can use flavoured dark chocolate if you like but try make sure the cocoa is 70% plus for a better richer flavour

You can add a topping!!!

250g milk or white chocolate melted and cooled to spreadable consistency

When the tiffin comes out of the fridge, set, pour over the chocolate mix and back in the fridge to set again for another 30 mins

# Rocky Roadish!

*My Version*

**Difficult rating:** ★★☆☆☆
**Serves:** 10
**Cooking time:** 10 mins
**Preparation time:** 20 mins
**Give Yourself Time:** 35 mins *(plus 2-3 hours in fridge to set)*

## You Will Need

*Weighing scales*
*Large saucepan*
*Measuring jug*
*Grease proof paper*
*Scissors*
*8 inch square cake tin*
*Tablespoon*
*Large mixing bowl*
*Spatula*
*Large metal spoon*
*Knife*
*Chopping board*

## Ingredients

- 75g coconut oil
- 100g gluten free dark chocolate (70% cocoa min) broken into chunks
- 3 tbspns of favourite seeds (sunflower, sesame, chia, linseed etc)
- 4 tbspns dried mixed fruit (raisins, cranberries etc)
- 3 tbspns cocoa powder
- 60g chopped mixed nuts (walnuts, almonds etc)
- 2 tbspns goji berries
- 50g chopped dried apricots
- 4 tbspns maple syrup

## Method

Line the cake time with the grease proof paper, covering the bottom and sides as best you can

KEY In the saucepan, add the coconut oil, maple syrup and dark chocolate and **melt gently** to combine using the spatula – **do not let it boil!**

Add all of the other ingredients and stir well with the spatula to ensure everything is combined and covered well

Put the mixture into the cake tin and push to the sides and as even a filling as you can get

Put into the fridge for 2-3 hours to set

When it is ready, remove from the tin and cut into the chunks size of your choice

### Hints & Tips

This will keep in an airtight container for a good week

### Ways To Change

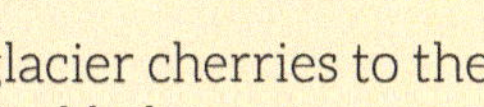

Add chopped glacier cherries to the mix for a bit of added sweetness

Mix up the nuts and/or seeds mixes to get to a combination you love

Try flavoured dark chocolate but try make sure it is 70% plus on the cocoa side

Use different mixed fruits, tropical ones give a totally different taste

# For Me and / or Family

# Filled Jacket Potatoes

*A simple one when need to plan ahead and a family fave most definitely!*

**Difficult rating:** ★★☆☆☆
**Serves:** As Many As You Need
**Cooking time:** 90 mins
**Preparation time:** 15 mins
**Give Yourself Time:** 120 mins

**You Will Need**

*Baking tray*
*Knife*
*Metal spoon*
*Chopping board*
*Large bowl*
*Tablespoon*

## Ingredients

- 4 baking potatoes
- 150ml milk – whole or semi
- 1 tbspn butter
- Grated cheese
- Salt and pepper

## Method

KEY Preheat the oven to 200c fan

KEY TIMER Put the potatoes on a tray and cook until can easily insert a skewer into the flesh (1hr – 1 ¼ hrs normally depending on the size)

KEY Remove the potatoes but **keep the oven on**

Cut each into halves completely separated – be careful as hot

Carefully scoop out the potato flesh of each into a separate large bowl, keeping the skins intact as best you can

Mash the potato as much as can before adding the milk and butter and seasoning

Combine to leave as few lumps as can

Add a handful of the grated cheese to the mix and carefully combine

Using a metal spoon, place the mixture back into each of the potato skin shells until just above the top of each

Top with some more grated cheese

KEY TIMER Return to the oven to bake until the topping is golden brown (around 15 mins)

## Hints & Tips

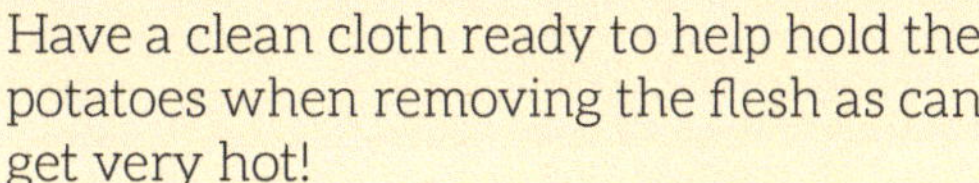

Have a clean cloth ready to help hold the potatoes when removing the flesh as can get very hot!

Use enough milk to make the mixture smooth but not sloppy

## Ways To Change

Add onion, chilli, mustard, corned beef, whatever you want to pimp it up. But remember you only have the same amount of shells to fill so don't overdo it!

Try different cheeses, flavoured etc.

Add some chopped chorizo to the topping

Use the Bolognese mix *(see recipe on page 51)* to top the cooked potatoes

Kids love baked beans mixed into the mashed potatoes too (and most adults!)

You could add tuna, mayo, sweetcorn

Put a bit of curry powder into the potato mix with some onion

# Potato Rosti

*Kids love this one, it's posh chips really!*

**Difficult rating:** ★★★☆☆
**Serves:** 4
**Cooking time:** 35 mins
**Preparation time:** 15 mins
**Give Yourself Time:** 60 mins

**You Will Need**

*Weighing scales*
*Large bowl*
*Knife*
*Chopping board*
*Large frying pan*
*Spatula*
*Potato peeler*
*Tablespoon*
*Colander / sieve*
*Grater*
*Large plate*

### Ingredients

- 1kg small baking potatoes (not peeled yet)
- 1 small white onion peeled and sliced (a cup of frozen works great too)
- 15g butter
- 2 tbspns rapeseed oil
- Salt and pepper

### Method

KEY TIMER Leave the potatoes whole and in their skins and cook in boiling salted water for **10mins until soft but not completely tender**

Drain and leave to cool

When cool enough to touch, peel the skins off the potatoes and coarsely grate into a large bowl

Stir in the onion and season with salt and pepper

Heat the butter and oil together in a non-stick frying pan

Tip the potato mixture into the pan and gently spread to an even layer

KEY TIMER Cook under a medium heat for 10 mins or until the edges are visibly golden

Shake the pan gently to loosen the potato mix, then with a plate over the top of the frying pan (top side down and bigger than the frying pan), invert the pan so the potato cake comes out

KEY TIMER Slide it back in now upside down into the pan and continue to fry for a further 10 mins

When brown underneath remove and serve

### Hints & Tips

Always make sure you have a plate ready for the flip before you start, and make sure it is bigger than the frying pan!

Get help if you need it as it can be messy otherwise!

### Ways To Change

Try adding grated cheese to the mixture for added goo

Cabbage and/or scallion (spring onion) give added flavour and crunch

Corned beef creates a hash type rosti

# Spinach & Rocket Tortilla

*Sounds hard – really isn't!*

**Difficult rating:** ★★★☆☆
**Serves:** 4-6
**Cooking time:** 30 mins
**Preparation time:** 15-20 mins
**Give Yourself Time:** 60 mins

## You Will Need

*Knife*
*Chopping board*
*Medium sauce pan*
*Large deep based frying pan*
*Mixing bowl*
*Whisk*
*Spatula*
*Teaspoon*
*Cup*

## Ingredients

- 500g new potatoes
- Rapeseed oil for frying
- 1 white onion, peeled and chopped (1 cup of frozen is ok too)
- 1 tspn chopped garlic (or one clove chopped)
- 8 free range eggs
- 2 handfuls of rocket chopped roughly
- 2 handfuls of spinach roughly chopped
- Salt & pepper
- (optional) 1 tspn chilli flakes

### Hints & Tips 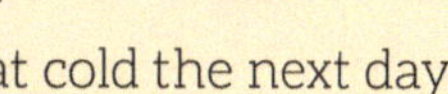

This is great cold the next day and will keep in the fridge

### Ways To Change

Add some herbs of your choice if you want to, either fresh coriander right at the end or dried herbs into the egg mix

## Method

KEY Turn the grill on now to high to heat up

KEY TIMER Cut the potatoes into 1/4s and cook in salted boiling water in the sauce pan for 15-20 mins until just cooked on the outside and a bit of bite in the middle

Drain the potatoes and leave to cool and dry out

KEY Heat the oil in the frying pan, add the onion and cook gently for 5 mins – **do not brown, just soften them slowly**

Add the garlic and continue to cook slowly for a further 2-3 minutes

KEY – **turn the heat up** under the frying pan and add the potatoes and chilli flakes (if using) and fry on a **medium heat** until the potato starts to brown at the edges

KEY **– turn the heat down to medium low** and add in the rocket and spinach and stir well

Break all of the eggs into the bowl, add a pinch of salt and pepper and whisk until smooth

Pour the egg mixture over the potato mix

Use your spatula to keep checking the edges of the egg aren't catching

KEY **Don't stir it – leave it untouched for 5minutes**

Carefully transfer the frying pan to underneath the grill – keep the handle pointing outwards and away from the direct heat

KEY TIMER grill for 5 mins until golden brown on top and no wobbly bits!

Very carefully remove the pan from the grill and put it on top of your hob.

KEY give the pan a good shake to ensure it is free at the edges and underneath, use your spatula if any areas need teasing away

Slide the tortilla out onto a board or plate to serve

Serve with a salad, warm or hot

# Potato, Broccoli & Bacon Tray Bake

*A surprising favourite in one dish*

**Difficult rating:** ★★★☆☆
**Serves:** 4-6
**Cooking time:** 45-50 mins
**Preparation time:** 15 mins
**Give Yourself Time:** 75 mins

### You Will Need

*Measuring jug*
*Cup*
*Knife*
*Chopping board*
*Large sauce pan*
*Colander / sieve*
*Large mixing bowl*
*Shallow cooking dish*

### Ingredients

- 1 small bag of new potatoes
- ¼ pint cream (single)
- 1 packet of un-smoked bacon
- Salt and pepper
- 1 packet of tender stem broccoli
- 1 cup of cherry tomatoes
- ½ packet of cream cheese (garlic and herb is best)
- ¼ pint milk (semi or whole)

### Hints & Tips

Don't overcook the potatoes or broccoli – in this undercooking is better at the early stage

Try and keep the tips of the broccoli under the cheese/milk mixture so it won't burn

### Ways To Change

Add cooked chicken strips before pouring over the cheese/milk mixture

Spice it up a bit with some grated chilli cheese on top

### Method

KEY Pre-heat the oven to 200c

Boil the potatoes in their skins until just cooked – firm

For the last 5 mins of boiling, add the broccoli until just cooked too

Drain and set aside

Cook the bacon how you wish – fry or oven bake but until nice and crispy

Cut into small bitesize pieces and set aside

Lay the potatoes and broccoli into a large oven baking dish, spreading evenly

Spread the bacon pieces and tomatoes evenly throughout

Season with salt and pepper

In a separate bowl, combine the cream cheese, milk and cream and mix thoroughly

Pour the mix over the potatoes and broccoli into the dish

KEY TIMER Bake for 40 mins

# Spaghetti Bolognese

*Never fails to be eaten up by everyone!*
*A great versatile one for the freezer too & the base for so many dishes (see later!)*

**Difficult rating:** ★★☆☆☆
**Serves:** 4-6
**Cooking time:** 35-40 mins
**Preparation time:** 15 mins
**Give Yourself Time:** 60 mins

### You Will Need

*Measuring jug*
*Knife*
*Chopping board*
*Large deep based frying pan*
*Can opener*
*Vegetable peeler*
*Weighing scales*
*Teaspoon*
*Tablespoon*
*Spatula*
*Tongues (grabbers!)*
*Cup (if frozen onion)*

### Ingredients

- 500g minced beef (I use 5% fat for health but use your preferred)
- 1 tbspn tomato puree
- 1 white onion chopped (or 1 cup frozen is great too)
- 2 tbspn gluten free Worcester sauce
- 2 carrots peeled and diced
- 1 bay leaf
- 1 tbspn garlic chopped
- 1 tbspn mixed Italian herbs
- 1 tbspn ginger chopped
- 400 ml beef stock (cube fine)
- 1 tin chopped tomatoes
- 100g per person of gluten free spaghetti
- Rapeseed oil for frying

### Hints & Tips

Don't rush the onions, time equals flavour

If you can also get the beef nicely coloured before you move on it will add flavour too

It is important to 'cook out' the tomato puree for a good 10 mins, which basically just means getting rid of the tinny flavour!

### Ways To Change

Adding cinnamon is my wife's favourite for a Middle Eastern kick

This recipe can be used and cooked in a batch, then into re-usable containers in your own portion sizes and frozen (once cold of course). It can then be used when you want.

There are a number of recipes to follow in this book that use this base mix to make so many other great dishes - great if you aren't feeling too clever as a kick start

### Method

Add the rapeseed oil to a large frying pan and heat on a medium

KEY TIMER Add the carrots and onions and fry for 5-10 mins, as long as your nerve will allow you

Turn up the heat to high and add the minced beef

KEY Break it up and brown the meat completely until juices run clear

Add the garlic and ginger to the pan and stir fully, reduce heat to medium

Add the Worcester sauce and stir through

KEY TIMER Add the tomato puree and make sure thoroughly combined – cook for at least 10 mins

Add the tin of tomatoes and the herbs and stir through

KEY TIMER Pour over the stock, add the bay leaf, seasoning, bring to the boil, then cover and simmer on a low heat for 25-30 mins, stirring occasionally

Cook the pasta according to the packet guidelines when you are ready to eat

Serve with gluten free garlic bread (see recipe on page 129) and some cheese on top of the bolognese!

# Beef Tacos

*A family fave for messy eaters!*

**Difficult rating:** ★★☆☆☆
**Serves:** 4-6
**Cooking time:** 15* mins
**Preparation time:** 5-7* mins
**Give Yourself Time:** 25* mins
**If making the beef mix from scratch then times will all increase*

## You Will Need

*Large saucepan*
*Teaspoon*
*Baking tray*
*Chopping board*
*Knife*

## Ingredients

- 500g Bolognese base beef mix (either cooked from scratch *(see recipe on page 51)* or a bag from the freezer already made
- ½ iceberg lettuce chopped into strips
- ½ tspn chilli flakes
- Bowl of grated cheese
- ½ tspn ground cumin
- Small tub sour cream or crème freche
- Hand-full of fresh coriander (chopped) or 2 tspns frozen
- Small tub guacamole *(see recipe on page 130)*
- 1 packet of gluten free corn taco shells

## Hints & Tips

KEY If you are using pre made beef mix from the freezer, make sure you take it out and put in the fridge overnight to defrost.

## Ways To Change

You can really spice it up with a lot more chilli if you can handle it

Add some refried beans (easily available in cans) or any beans of your choice to the beef mix really can change the flavour and excitement!

## Method

KEY – preheat the oven to 180C for the taco shells

Make up the Bolognese mix *(see recipe on page 51)*, or

Add the defrosted bag of ready made Bolognese to a pan to warm through

Add the chilli flakes, cumin and coriander and stir through as it warms up

KEY TIMER Put the taco shells onto the baking tray and cook as per the packet instructions

Put the shredded lettuce, grated cheese, sour cream or crème freche and guacamole into separate serving bowls

When the beef mix is nice and hot, serve along with the taco shells and all of the accompaniments

Enjoy building your tacos how you like in whatever order you like!

# Cheesy Topped Cottage Pie

*No Shepherds Here!*

**Difficult rating:** ★★★☆☆
**Serves:** 4-6
**Cooking time:** 60* mins
**Preparation time:** 30-40* mins
**Give Yourself Time:** 110* mins
**If making this with ready-made beef mix then times will reduce*

## You Will Need

*Large saucepan*
*Knife*
*Chopping board*
*Weighing scales*
*Large metal spoon*
*Measuring jug*
*Potato peeler*
*Masher*
*Colander / sieve*
*Large oven / serving dish*

## Ingredients

- 500g Bolognese base beef mix (either cooked from scratch *(see recipe on page 51)* or a bag from the freezer already made
- 90ml milk
- 700g maris piper potatoes peeled and chopped
- Salt & pepper
- 1 large knob butter
- 100g grated cheddar cheese (keep 20g for the topping)

## Method

KEY preheat the oven to 200C

Put the chopped potatoes into a large pan of salted boiling water

Cook until you can get a knife easily through the potato pieces (time depends on what size they are)

Drain the potatoes through a colander / sieve and return to the pan

KEY keep the hob on underneath the pan at a medium/low heat

Add the milk, butter and salt and pepper to the potatoes and mash well until smooth and creamy

Stir in 80g of the grated cheese and combine well

Put the prepared beef mince base into the bottom of the oven dish and spread evenly

Carefully spoon over the mashed potato so is covered evenly

Sprinkle the remaining 20g cheese over the top and put into the oven

KEY TIMER Bake for 35-40 minutes until the top is nice and brown

## Hints & Tips

When putting mashed potato on top of any mix for the oven, if you start putting it on from the outsides first and working your way in, it means that any liquid within the sauce isn't pushed over the sides.

## Ways To Change

Spice it up a bit with some chilli flakes

Try different cheeses within the mash and on top

Try adding some whole grain mustard to the mash (1-2 tspns) for some interesting heat

# Chilli Beef & Rice

*Never fails to impress*

**Difficult rating:** ★★☆☆☆
**Serves:** 4-6
**Cooking time:** 15-20* mins
**Preparation time:** 10* mins
**Give Yourself Time:** 40* mins
**If making the beef mix from scratch then times will all increase*

### You Will Need

*1 large saucepan with lid*
*1 medium saucepan*
*Teaspoon*
*Colander / sieve*

### Ingredients

- 500g Bolognese base beef mix (either cooked from scratch *(see recipe on page 51)* or a bag from the freezer already made
- Rice – volume depends on packet / box instructions
- 1 tspn dried oregano
- 1 tspn dried chilli flakes
- 1 tspn dried coriander
- 1 can red kidney beans – drained
- 1 small tub sour cream of crème freche

### Hints & Tips

If the beef mix is a bit dry, add some water or a bit more beef stock

Make sure you have taken the beef mix out of the freezer the night before to defrost in the fridge

### Ways To Change 

Use mixed beans instead of just kidney beans

Chilli beans are great for some fire

Add 1 tspn of smoked paprika for a smokey fire

Using different types of rice, wholegrain

### Method

Make up the Bolognese mix *(see recipe on page 51)*, or

Add the defrosted bag of ready made Bolognese to a large sauce pan

KEY TIMER Add all of the herbs and spices and the kidney beans, lid on and simmer for 15-20 minutes

Cook the rice according to the packet instructions

Serve when both piping hot

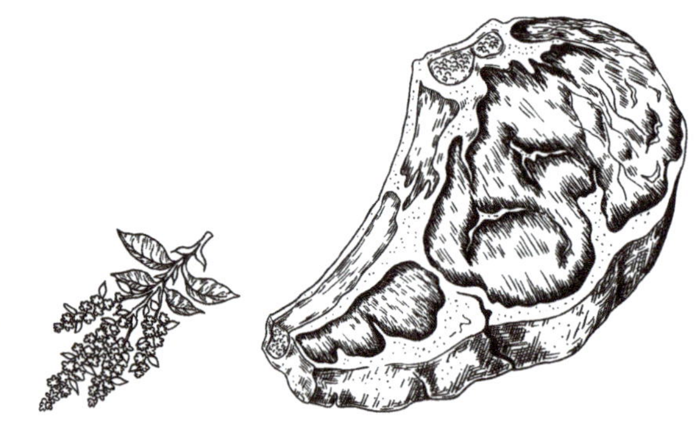

# Minced Beef Lasagne

*Never fails to impress*

**Difficult rating:** ★★★☆☆
**Serves:** 4-6
**Cooking time:** 25-30* mins
**Preparation time:** 25* mins
**Give Yourself Time:** 50-60* mins
**If making the beef mix from scratch then times will all increase*

## You Will Need

*Large deep cooking / serving dish*
*Measuring scales*
*Measuring jug*
*Large saucepan*
*Wooden spoon*
*Whisk*
*Tablespoon*
*Teaspoon*

## Ingredients

- 500g Bolognese base beef mix (either cooked from scratch (see recipe on page 51) or a bag from the freezer already made
- 4 tbspns gluten free plain flour
- 50g butter
- 500ml milk (full or half fat best)
- 150g grated cheddar cheese (50g retained for top)
- 1 packet gluten free lasagne sheets

## Hints & Tips

Give the cheese sauce your full attention and stay with it throughout!

You have to keep stirring and adding, stirring and adding, or you will end up with a very lumpy sauce

## Ways To Change

Add a tspn of English mustard to the cheese sauce when the cheese goes in

Add a tspn of grated nutmeg to the sauce when the cheese goes in

## Method

KEY pre heat the oven to 200C

Make up the Bolognese mix, (see recipe on page 51) or

Have the defrosted bag of ready-made Bolognese ready to go

KEY In the saucepan, gently melt the butter (**not boiling or fizzing**)

KEY When all is melted, add the gluten free plain flour and **keep stirring**

Keep stirring until a thick wallpaper type paste is there

KEY turn the heat up under the pan to medium

KEY Slowly start adding the milk, **dribbles at a time** and **KEEP STIRRING**

KEY After each milk amount goes in**, stir like mad and get out any lumps** you can see before adding the milk again. It will go thick and gloopy again until enough milk is combined

Keep going until all of the milk is in and there are no lumps

Use the whisk if you can't get any lumps out

Keep stirring until the mix starts to thicken and coats the back of a wooden spoon when you lift it out

KEY take the pan off the heat and add 100g of the grated cheese and stir well to combine

In the oven dish, add half of the beef mix to the bottom and spread evenly

Put a single layer of the lasagne sheets over the beef mix

Add the remainder of the beef mix and evenly spread

Put another single layer of lasagne sheets over the beef

Pour over the entire pan of cheese sauce

Top with the remaining 50g of grated cheese

KEY TIMER bake in the oven for 25-30 mins until is golden brown on top and a knife easily passes through the pasta sheets

Carefully remove and serve with a salad or chips or wedges (see recipe on page 135) and garlic bread (see recipe on page 129)

# Beef Burritos

*A Mexican Lasagne!*

**Difficult rating:** ★★☆☆☆
**Serves:** 4-6
**Cooking time:** 15* mins
**Preparation time:** 15* mins
**Give Yourself Time:** 40* mins

**If making the beef mix from scratch then times will all increase*

### You Will Need

*Large cooking / serving deep dish*
*Large saucepan*
*Chopping board*
*Metal spoon*
*Teaspoon*
*Cup*

### Ingredients

- 500g Bolognese base beef mix (either cooked from *(see recipe on page 51)* or a bag from the freezer already made
- 6-8 gluten free tortilla wraps
- 2 Cups grated cheese (keep some back for serving)
- 2 Cups tomato salsa
- ½ tspn ground cumin
- Small tub sour cream or crème freche
- Small tub guacamole *(see recipe on page 130)*
- ½ tspn chilli flakes

### Hints & Tips

Make sure you have taken the beef mix out of the freezer the night before to defrost in the fridge

### Ways To Change

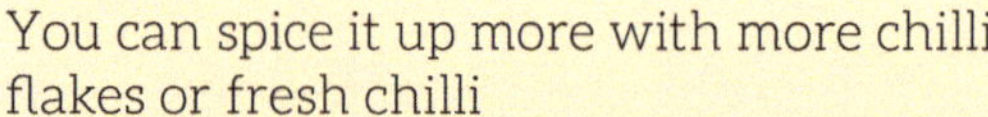

You can spice it up more with more chilli flakes or fresh chilli

Add some cooked rice to the rolled up beef mixes

### Method

**KEY** pre heat the oven to 200C

Make up the Bolognese mix *(see recipe on page 51)*, or

Have the defrosted bag of ready made Bolognese ready to go

Stir in the ground cumin and chilli flakes to the beef mix (it is ok if it is cold when doing this)

Put a tortilla wrap on the chopping board

Carefully spoon some of the beef mixture on one side of the wrap all the way down

Carefully roll up the wrap, from the full side across, until fully rolled.

Place the filled wrap into the cooking dish so it fits top to bottom

Repeat with all of the wraps until the dish is full

Dribble the salsa over the top of the wraps so it is mostly covered but some peeking through (as will go nice and crispy)

Sprinkle over the grated cheese

**KEY TIMER** bake in the oven for 15 mins and the cheese is brown and the salsa bubbling

Put the sour cream / crème freche, guacamole and cheese into separate servicing bowls

Serve and enjoy with a nice salad

# Burgers!

*Yes, you can buy these, but there is nothing better than your own!*

## Start with The Basic One

**Difficult rating:** ★☆☆☆☆
**Serves:** 4-6
**Cooking time:** 10-15 mins
**Preparation time:** 15 mins
**Give Yourself Time:** 35 mins

**You Will Need**

*Large frying pan or griddle pan if you have*
*Large mixing bowl*
*Baking tray lined with grease proof paper (scissors to cut)*
*Spatula*
*Tablespoon*
*Gluten free rolls*

### Ingredients

- 500g minced beef (10% fat for flavour, 5% fat if health conscious)
- Salt & pepper
- 2 Tbspns rapeseed oil

### Method

Put all of the mince into the mixing bowl

Add a pinch of salt & pepper

Mix well with your hands to combine (honestly, hands are best, just make sure you washed them first!)

Shape pieces into burger sizes you want – I find about 3 inches wide and ½ inch thick is easiest

KEY Put each onto the lined baking tray and when done all of them put them into the fridge for a minimum of 5 mins. This helps them firm up and not fall apart when cooking

Remove the burgers from the fridge when ready to cook

Heat the oil in the frying pan under a medium heat

Fry the burgers, turning regularly, until brown on both sides and cooked as you like inside.

KEY 5 mins each side will give you a medium burger – just a guide as depends on how thick you have your burgers

Serve in gluten free rolls with salad and wedges *(see recipe on page 135)*

### Hints & Tips

You can freeze the burgers when shaped, so before 'go into the fridge' part, and keep them for another day – great to be ahead of the game, just remember to defrost thoroughly in the fridge before cooking

To save you guessing, a meat thermometer is a fantastic thing to have and they cost really very little. Each one will have a guide with it as to how your meat is cooked, saving you having to chop some apart to check!

### Ways To Change

The following pages give you different flavoured burgers you can try – enjoy!

# Onion, Garlic & Chilli Burger

**Difficult rating:** ★★☆☆☆
**Serves:** 4-6
**Cooking time:** 10-15 mins
**Preparation time:** 15 mins
**Give Yourself Time:** 35 mins

**You Will Need**

*Large frying pan or griddle pan if you have*
*Large mixing bowl*
*Baking tray lined with grease proof paper (scissors to cut)*
*Spatula*
*Tablespoon*
*Gluten free rolls*
*Teaspoon*

### Ingredients

- 500g minced beef (10% fat for flavour, 5% fat if health conscious)
- Salt & pepper
- 2 Tbspns rapeseed oil
- ½ white onion chopped finely (1/2 cup frozen works too)
- 1 tspn chopped garlic (1 clove fine)
- 1 tspn dried chilli flakes

### Hints & Tips

You can freeze the burgers when shaped, so before 'go into the fridge' part, and keep them for another day - great to be ahead of the game, just remember to defrost thoroughly in the fridge before cooking

To save you guessing, a meat thermometer is a fantastic thing to have and they cost really very little. Each one will have a guide with it as to how your meat is cooked, saving you having to chop some apart to check!

### Method

Put all of the mince into the mixing bowl

Add a pinch of salt & pepper

KEY In the frying pan, gently fry the onion, garlic and chilli until just about to brown (about 10 mins on medium heat)

Add onion, garlic and chilli mix to the beef

Mix well with your hands (careful as may be a bit hot!) to combine (honestly, hands are best, just make sure you washed them first!)

Shape pieces into burger sizes you want - I find about 3 inches wide and ½ inch thick is easiest

KEY Put each onto the lined baking tray and when done all of them put them into the fridge for a minimum of 5 mins. This helps them firm up and not fall apart when cooking

Remove the burgers from the fridge when ready to cook

Heat the oil in the frying pan under a medium heat

Fry the burgers, turning regularly, until brown on both sides and cooked as you like inside.

KEY 5 mins each side will give you a medium burger - just a guide as depends on how thick you have your burgers

Serve in gluten free rolls with salad and wedges *(see recipe on page 135)*

# Lemon & Herby Burger

**Difficult rating:** ★★☆☆☆
**Serves:** 4-6
**Cooking time:** 10-15 mins
**Preparation time:** 15 mins
**Give Yourself Time:** 35 mins

## You Will Need

*Large frying pan or griddle pan if you have*
*Large mixing bowl*
*Baking tray lined with grease proof paper (scissors to cut)*
*Spatula*
*Tablespoon*
*Gluten free rolls*
*Teaspoon*

## Ingredients

- 500g minced beef (10% fat for flavour, 5% fat if health conscious)
- Salt & pepper
- 2 Tbspns rapeseed oil (for frying)
- ½ tspn dried chopped rosemary
- ½ tspn dried chopped thyme
- Zest of one whole lemon
- Juice of half the lemon
- 1 Tbspn extra virgin olive oil

## Hints & Tips

You can freeze the burgers when shaped, so before 'go into the fridge' part, and keep them for another day - great to be ahead of the game, just remember to defrost thoroughly in the fridge before cooking

To save you guessing, a meat thermometer is a fantastic thing to have and they cost really very little. Each one will have a guide with it as to how your meat is cooked, saving you having to chop some apart to check!

## Method

Put all of the mince into the mixing bowl

Add a pinch of salt & pepper

Add all of the herbs, olive oil and the lemon zest and juice to the beef

Mix well with your hands to combine (honestly, hands are best, just make sure you washed them first!)

Shape pieces into burger sizes you want – I find about 3 inches wide and ½ inch thick is easiest

KEY Put each onto the lined baking tray and when done all of them put them into the fridge for a minimum of 5 mins. This helps them firm up and not fall apart when cooking

Remove the burgers from the fridge when ready to cook

Heat the oil in the frying pan under a medium heat

Fry the burgers, turning regularly, until brown on both sides and cooked as you like inside.

KEY 5 mins each side will give you a medium burger – just a guide as depends on how thick you have your burgers

Serve in gluten free rolls with salad and wedges *(see recipe on page 135)*

# Mexican Style Burger

**Difficult rating:** ★★☆☆☆
**Serves:** 4-6
**Cooking time:** 10-15 mins
**Preparation time:** 15 mins
**Give Yourself Time:** 35 mins

## You Will Need

*Large frying pan or griddle pan if you have*
*Large mixing bowl*
*Baking tray lined with grease proof paper (scissors to cut)*
*Spatula*
*Tablespoon*
*Gluten free rolls*
*Teaspoon*
*Small mixing bowl*

## Ingredients

- 500g minced beef (10% fat for flavour, 5% fat if health conscious)
- Salt & pepper
- 2 Tbspns rapeseed oil (for frying)
- ½ tspn ground cumin
- ½ tspn ground coriander
- ½ tspn chilli flakes
- ½ tspn smoked paprika
- 1 Tbspn extra virgin olive oil

## Hints & Tips

You can freeze the burgers when shaped, so before 'go into the fridge' part, and keep them for another day - great to be ahead of the game, just remember to defrost thoroughly in the fridge before cooking

To save you guessing, a meat thermometer is a fantastic thing to have and they cost really very little. Each one will have a guide with it as to how your meat is cooked, saving you having to chop some apart to check!

## Method

Put all of the mince into the mixing bowl

Add a pinch of salt & pepper

Add all of the spices, herbs and olive oil to the beef

Mix well with your hands to combine (honestly, hands are best, just make sure you washed them first!)

Shape pieces into burger sizes you want – I find about 3 inches wide and ½ inch thick is easiest

KEY Put each onto the lined baking tray and when done all of them put them into the fridge for a minimum of 5 mins. This helps them firm up and not fall apart when cooking

Remove the burgers from the fridge when ready to cook

Heat the oil in the frying pan under a medium heat

Fry the burgers, turning regularly, until brown on both sides and cooked as you like inside.

KEY 5 mins each side will give you a medium burger – just a guide as depends on how thick you have your burgers

Serve in gluten free rolls with salad and wedges *(see recipe on page 135)*

# Beef & Chilli Bean Burger

**Difficult rating:** ★★☆☆☆
**Serves:** 4-6
**Cooking time:** 10-15 mins
**Preparation time:** 15 mins
**Give Yourself Time:** 35 mins

## You Will Need

*Large frying pan or griddle pan if you have*
*Large mixing bowl*
*Baking tray lined with grease proof paper (scissors to cut)*
*Spatula*
*Tablespoon*
*Gluten free rolls*
*Teaspoon*
*Small mixing bowl*

## Ingredients

- 500g minced beef (10% fat for flavour, 5% fat if health conscious)
- Salt & pepper
- 2 Tbspns rapeseed oil (for frying)
- 1 small can of mixed chilli beans (drained)
- 1 tspn dried oregano
- 1 tspn dried ground coriander
- 1 Tbspn extra virgin olive oil

## Hints & Tips

You can freeze the burgers when shaped, so before 'go into the fridge' part, and keep them for another day - great to be ahead of the game, just remember to defrost thoroughly in the fridge before cooking

To save you guessing, a meat thermometer is a fantastic thing to have and they cost really very little. Each one will have a guide with it as to how your meat is cooked, saving you having to chop some apart to check!

## Method

Put all of the mince into the mixing bowl

Add a pinch of salt & pepper

Put the drained beans into the small mixing bowl

With the back of a spoon, gently squash the beans up a bit, roughly and not into a paste

Add all of the beans, herbs and olive oil to the beef

Mix well with your hands to combine (honestly, hands are best, just make sure you washed them first!)

Shape pieces into burger sizes you want - I find about 3 inches wide and ½ inch thick is easiest

KEY Put each onto the lined baking tray and when done all of them put them into the fridge for a minimum of 5 mins. This helps them firm up and not fall apart when cooking

Remove the burgers from the fridge when ready to cook

Heat the oil in the frying pan under a medium heat

Fry the burgers, turning regularly, until brown on both sides and cooked as you like inside.

KEY 5 mins each side will give you a medium burger - just a guide as depends on how thick you have your burgers

Serve in gluten free rolls with salad and wedges (see recipe on page 135)

# Hidden Cheese Burger

**Difficult rating:** ★★★☆☆
**Serves:** 4-6
**Cooking time:** 10-15 mins
**Preparation time:** 15 mins
**Give Yourself Time:** 35 mins

**You Will Need**

*Large frying pan or griddle pan if you have*
*Large mixing bowl*
*Baking tray lined with grease proof paper (scissors to cut)*
*Spatula*
*Tablespoon*
*Gluten free rolls*
*Teaspoon*

## Ingredients

- 500g minced beef (10% fat for flavour, 5% fat if health conscious)
- Salt & pepper
- 2 Tbspns rapeseed oil (for frying)
- 1 × mozzarella ball or
- a slice of brie, or
- a small tub of soft cream cheese

## Method

Put all of the mince into the mixing bowl

Add a pinch of salt & pepper

Mix well with your hands to combine (honestly, hands are best, just make sure you washed them first!)

When shaping the burgers and before flattening them out, make a small cup shape with the beef mix in your hand

Add 1p size pieces of the cheese into the well

Shape the burger meat around the cheese and gently flatten out so the cheese is hidden inside

Shape pieces into burger sizes you want – I find about 3 inches wide and ½ inch thick is easiest

**KEY** Put each onto the lined baking tray and when done all of them put them into the fridge for a minimum of 5 mins. This helps them firm up and not fall apart when cooking

Remove the burgers from the fridge when ready to cook

Heat the oil in the frying pan under a medium heat

Fry the burgers, turning regularly, until brown on both sides and cooked as you like inside.

**KEY** 5 mins each side will give you a medium burger – just a guide as depends on how thick you have your burgers

Serve in gluten free rolls with salad and wedges (see recipe on page 135)

## Hints & Tips

You can freeze the burgers when shaped, so before 'go into the fridge' part, and keep them for another day – great to be ahead of the game, just remember to defrost thoroughly in the fridge before cooking

To save you guessing, a meat thermometer is a fantastic thing to have and they cost really very little. Each one will have a guide with it as to how your meat is cooked, saving you having to chop some apart to check!

If the cheese oozes out when frying, it's absolutely fine! It just adds more texture and flavour

# Pork Burger

**Difficult rating:** ★★☆☆☆
**Serves:** 4-6
**Cooking time:** 15 mins
**Preparation time:** 15 mins
**Give Yourself Time:** 35 mins

## You Will Need

*Large frying pan or griddle pan if you have*
*Large mixing bowl*
*Baking tray lined with grease proof paper (scissors to cut)*
*Spatula*
*Tablespoon*
*Gluten free rolls*
*Teaspoon*

## Ingredients

- 500g minced pork
- Salt & pepper
- 1 free range egg
- 1 tspn paprika
- 1 tspn smoked paprika
- 1 tspn chopped garlic (one clove)
- 1 tspn dried mixed herbs
- 2 tbspns rapeseed oil for frying

## Hints & Tips

You can freeze the burgers when shaped, so before 'go into the fridge' part, and keep them for another day - great to be ahead of the game, just remember to defrost thoroughly in the fridge before cooking

To save you guessing, a meat thermometer is a fantastic thing to have and they cost really very little. Each one will have a guide with it as to how your meat is cooked, saving you having to chop some apart to check!

## Method

Beat the egg in the large bowl

Add all of the herbs and spices into the egg and combine well

Put all of the mince into the egg mix

Add a pinch of salt & pepper

Mix well with your hands to combine (honestly, hands are best, just make sure you washed them first!)

Shape pieces into burger sizes you want – I find about 3 inches wide and ½ inch thick is easiest

KEY Put each onto the lined baking tray and when done all of them put them into the fridge for a minimum of 5 mins. This helps them firm up and not fall apart when cooking

Remove the burgers from the fridge when ready to cook

Heat the oil in the frying pan under a medium heat

Fry the burgers, until brown on both sides and cooked as you like inside.

KEY 6-7 mins each side, just need to turn once (if you have thicker burgers please check they are cooked through using a meat thermometer

Serve in gluten free rolls with salad and wedges *(see recipe on page 135)*

# Corn, Chilli & Chickpea Burger

*Great meat alternative – not just for vegetarians*

**Difficult rating:** ★★☆☆☆
**Serves:** 4-6
**Cooking time:** 8 mins
**Preparation time:** 20 mins
**Give Yourself Time:** 35 mins

**You Will Need**

*Large frying pan or griddle pan if you have*
*Large mixing bowl*
*Spatula*
*Knife*
*Chopping board*
*Blender*
*Cup*

**Ingredients**

- 180g frozen sweetcorn
- 525g can of chickpeas, drained
- ½ white onion chopped finely (or ½ cup frozen)
- ½ teaspoon chopped garlic
- ½ cup frozen mixed peppers or chopped fresh
- 50g gluten free breadcrumbs (use GF white bread in a blender quickly or buy pre made)
- ½ lemon zested and juice
- ½ tspn dried thyme
- ½ tspn dried chilli flakes
- 4 tbspns corn flour
- Salt & pepper
- 2 Tbspns rapeseed oil for frying

**Hints & Tips**

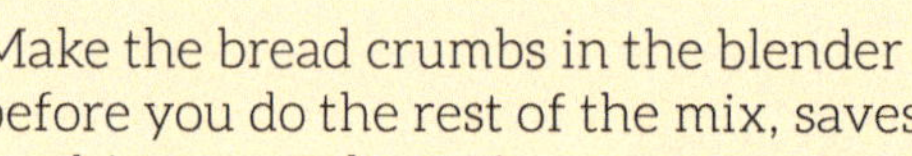

Make the bread crumbs in the blender first before you do the rest of the mix, saves washing up and mess!

Use the same frying pan as for the onions when frying the burgers, saves washing and adds flavour

**Method**

Heat ½ of the rapeseed oil in the frying pan on a medium heat

Add the onion, garlic, chilli, sweetcorn and thyme and fry gently for 2-3 mins

In a blender put in the chickpeas, breadcrumbs and half of the corn flour, salt and pepper and mix well

Add the onion mix to the blended chickpeas and pulse a few times so combined but not smooth

Tip the mixture into the mixing bowl

Shape into burger sizes of your choice

Heat the remaining rapeseed oil in the frying pan (and use the same pan from the onions as flavour in there and saves washing up too!)

Before frying, gently pat the remaining cornflour onto each side of your burgers and shake off any excess

**KEY TIMER** Cook on a medium heat for 4 mins each side until golden brown

Serve as you would any burger, in a gluten free bun with salad and wedges

# Whole Poached Chicken

*This is the Mr Versatile as can be used for anything*
*You won't go back once you've tried it!*

**Difficult rating:** ★★★☆☆
**Serves:** 4-6 (and the rest!)
**Cooking time:** 90 mins
**Preparation time:** 15 mins
**Give Yourself Time:** 120 mins

### You Will Need

*Large Saucepan or pot with lid (enough to take the whole chicken!)*
*Knife*
*Chopping board*
*Veg peeler*
*Tablespoon*
*Roasting tin*

### Ingredients

- 1 whole chicken (free range best) and make sure is empty!
- A sprig of fresh herbs – thyme and sage (a tbsp. of dried is fine also)
- 2-3 carrots peeled and chopped into bitesize chunks
- 1 tbsp. sea salt
- 1 large white onion peeled and roughly chopped
- Small new potatoes - optional
- 2-3 celery stalks peeled and roughly chopped
- 1 tbsp. whole black peppercorns
- 1-2 bay leaves

### Hints & Tips

Make sure you have the right size pot before starting, it's very messy otherwise!

Keep that broth!

### Ways To Change

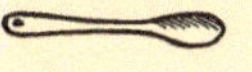

You could just pull the chicken apart and serve with the veg and the broth

Or you could strain the broth and keep it for soups and stocks, it freezes very well

You could add some rice noodles to the broth and chicken and have some chicken noodle soup!

### Method

Put the whole chicken into a large pot for the hob that has a lid and water can cover it completely

Add the onion, carrots, celery, peppercorns, garlic and herbs

Cover the chicken with cold water and add the salt

Bring to the boil then cover and simmer

KEY TIMER Use a tight-fitting lid and simmer for 1hr 20 mins

KEY Do not let this boil, it is a poach

KEY TIMER Turn off the heat, remove the chicken and transfer to a large roasting pan to cool for 20 mins

Save the broth and the vegetables as liquid gold!

KEY If adding the potatoes, add to the pot with about 30 mins to go

# Whole Roast Chicken Dinner

*Every Sunday Is Great With This One – Kids Love It*

**Difficult rating:** ★★★☆☆
**Serves:** 4-6
**Cooking time:** 2 hours
**Preparation time:** 30 mins
**Give Yourself Time:** 165 mins

**You Will Need**

*Knife*
*Chopping board*
*Measuring jug*
*Measuring scales*
*Whisk*
*Baking tray*
*Yorkshire pudding tin – 12 holes*
*Steamer (or saucepan if no steamer available)*

### Ingredients

- 1 × whole chicken (free range and giblets removed)
- Spiced red cabbage *(see recipe on page 144)*
- 6 × maris piper potatoes peeled and halved
- 2 × lemons
- 4 × carrots peeled and into batons
- Salt & Pepper
- 1 × packet purple sprouting broccoli
- Rapeseed oil
- Gluten free gravy granules
- Butter spray or room temp butter
- 12 × gluten free Yorkshire puddings *(see recipe on page 143)*

### Hints & Tips

Timing is everything! Take the longest item first, the chicken, add all the timings up for cooking and resting and work backwards as to what to do when. Keep it written down until it comes second nature

Always read the label on the chicken as to how long it takes to cook, each one is different

### Ways To Change

Add some fresh herbs to the inside of the chicken with the lemons, coriander and thyme are lovely

Add some whole garlic cloves inside too for some added flavour

### Method

KEY Pre heat the oven to 200c, making sure room for 3 trays including the chicken

Prepare the chicken (ideally at room temp) by spraying butter onto the skin all over, or rubbing in a knob of butter

Scatter sea salt onto the skin

Zest one of the lemons and scatter onto the chicken skin too

Cut the 2 lemons in half, pouring the juice of one over the skin too

Put the other 2 lemon halves into the chicken cavity

KEY TIMER Cook the chicken, uncovered, as per the package instructions for the size, **leaving 10mins extra to rest**

Place the potato halves onto a baking tray, sprinkle with sea salt and pour over rapeseed oil to coat. Toss them to ensure completely covered and place on their flattest edge

KEY TIMER When the chicken has 1 hour to go, put the potatoes in to cook

**KEY** Make the Yorkshire pudding mix as per the recipe and leave to stand for at least 20 mins before using

**KEY TIMER** When there are 30 mins to go for the potatoes and chicken, put a drop of rapeseed oil into the bottom of each of a 12 hole yorkie tin and put it into the oven for 5 mins

**KEY TIMER** Make sure you have the yorkie mix in a pouring jug. Remove the hot tin and oil from the oven (be very careful as seriously hot oil). Pour in the mix to each hole and return to the oven for 25 mins

**KEY TIMER** in a steamer, put the carrot batons in the bottom layer and season with salt, and start with 20 mins to go until the potatoes and chicken are ready

**KEY TIMER** Put the broccoli in, season, to the top layer with 10 mins to go

If you don't have a steamer just use a pan of salted boiling water

The spiced cabbage can be made ahead, kept in the fridge or even frozen, then heated up when needed

Make the gravy as per the instructions – make it nice and thick!

**KEY TIMER** Remove the chicken, cover with foil and leave to rest for 10 mins

When the chicken is removed, put a few serving dishes in the oven to heat up

Remove everything from the oven, put into serving dishes and enjoy!

# Basic Creamy Curry

*Ready for Anything*
*Great recipe ideas following.....*

**Difficult rating:** ★★★☆☆
**Serves:** min 4
**Cooking time:** 20 mins
**Preparation time:** 15 mins
**Give Yourself Time:** 40 mins

**You Will Need**

Large deep frying pan
Knife
Chopping board
Large plastic or metal mixing spoon
Cup
Teaspoon
Tablespoon

### Ingredients

- 1 white onion, peeled and chopped (a cup of frozen is fine too)
- 1 tspn chopped garlic
- 1 tspn chopped ginger
- 1 heaped tspn curry powder (your choice of heat)
- 1 heaped tspn garam masala
- 1 cup frozen sliced mixed peppers or ½ red and ½ yellow fresh sliced
- 4 tbspns plain natural yoghurt
- 250ml vegetable stock (from a cube ok)
- 2 tbspns rapeseed oil for frying
- Handful of fresh coriander, torn into bits

### Method

On a medium heat, add the rapeseed oil to the frying pan

KEY TIMER add the onion and slowly cook it, not flash frying! 10 mins minimum but as long as you can go!

KEY TIMER Add the ginger, garlic, curry powder, garam masala and sliced peppers and continue to cook for another 5 minutes

Stir in the yoghurt and add the stock, stirring until well combined

KEY TIMER Let it slowly simmer away for another 5-10 mins but not boil too vigorously

Just before serving add the fresh coriander and mix in

Ready to serve as you wish

**This is great poured over cooked chicken or fish, or you can poach some fish as per the poached chicken recipe.**

**You can really go to town on what you add, as per the following recipes using this as the base for the curry**

# Fried Chicken Creamy Curry

*Kids love this one!*

**Difficult rating:** ★★★☆☆
**Serves:** min 4
**Cooking time:** 20 mins
**Preparation time:** 15 mins
**Give Yourself Time:** 40 mins

**You Will Need**

*Large deep frying pan*
*Knife*
*Chopping board*
*Large plastic or metal mixing spoon*
*Cup*
*Teaspoon*
*Tablespoon*

## Ingredients

- 1 white onion, peeled and chopped (a cup of frozen is fine too)
- 1 tspn chopped garlic
- 1 tspn chopped ginger
- 1 heaped tspn curry powder (your choice of heat)
- 1 heaped tspn garam masala
- 1 cup frozen sliced mixed peppers or ½ red and ½ yellow fresh sliced
- 4 tbspns plain natural yoghurt
- 250ml vegetable stock (from a cube ok)
- 2 tbspns rapeseed oil for frying
- 1 packet of raw chicken strips, or 2 breasts cut into slices
- Handful of fresh coriander torn into bits

## Method

On a medium heat, add the rapeseed oil to the frying pan

KEY TIMER add the onion and slowly cook it, not flash frying! 10 mins minimum but as long as you can go!

Add the chicken strips and cook until they are starting to brown and cooked through (use a meat thermometer if not sure but quickly cutting into one will tell you)

KEY TIMER Add the ginger, garlic, curry powder, garam masala and sliced peppers and continue to cook for another 5 minutes

Stir in the yoghurt and add the stock, stirring until well combined

KEY TIMER Let it slowly simmer away for another 5-10 mins but not boil too vigorously

Just before service add in the fresh coriander and mix in

Ready to serve as you wish

# Poached Chicken Creamy Curry

*Kids love this one aswell!*
*Just a bit softer*

**Difficult rating:** ★★★☆☆
**Serves:** min 4
**Cooking time:** 20 mins
**Preparation time:** 15 mins
**Give Yourself Time:** 40 mins

**You Will Need**

*Large deep frying pan*
*Knife*
*Chopping board*
*Large plastic or metal mixing spoon*
*Cup*
*Teaspoon*
*Tablespoon*

## Ingredients

- 1 white onion, peeled and chopped (a cup of frozen is fine too)
- 1 tspn chopped garlic
- 1 tspn chopped ginger
- 1 heaped tspn curry powder (your choice of heat)
- 1 heaped tspn garam masala
- 1 cup frozen sliced mixed peppers or ½ red and ½ yellow fresh sliced
- 4 tbspns plain natural yoghurt
- 250ml vegetable stock (from a cube ok)
- 2 tbspns rapeseed oil for frying
- 1 packet of raw chicken strips, or 2 breasts cut into slices
- Handful of fresh coriander torn into bits

## Method

On a medium heat, add the rapeseed oil to the frying pan

KEY TIMER add the onion and slowly cook it, not flash frying! 10 mins minimum but as long as you can go!

KEY TIMER Add the ginger, garlic, curry powder, garam masala and sliced peppers and continue to cook for another 5 minutes

Stir in the yoghurt and add the stock, stirring until well combined

Add the chicken strips and allow to poach in the sauce

KEY TIMER Let it slowly simmer away for another 10 mins but not boil too vigorously, and the chicken is cooked through

Just before service, add in the fresh coriander and mix in

Ready to serve as you wish

# Tandoori Style Chicken Creamy Curry

*A great twist!*

**Difficult rating:** ★★★☆☆
**Serves:** min 4
**Cooking time:** 20 mins
**Preparation time:** 45 mins
**Give Yourself Time:** 40 mins

## You Will Need

*Large deep frying pan*
*Knife*
*Chopping board*
*Large plastic or metal mixing spoon*
*Cup*
*Teaspoon*
*Tablespoon*
*Re-usable freezer container*

## Ingredients

- 1 white onion, peeled and chopped (a cup of frozen is fine too)
- 1 tspn chopped garlic
- 1 tspn chopped ginger
- 1 heaped tspn curry powder (your choice of heat)
- 1 heaped tspn garam masala
- 1 cup frozen sliced mixed peppers or ½ red and ½ yellow fresh sliced
- 4 tbspns plain natural yoghurt
- 250ml vegetable stock (from a cube ok)
- 2 tbspns rapeseed oil for frying
- 1 packet of raw chicken strips, or 2 breasts cut into slices
- 1 tbspn tandoori dried spice
- Handful of fresh coriander torn into bits

## Method

Half an hour before (minimum, longer better) put the chicken strips into the freezer container, add the tandoori spice and then half of the yoghurt, so 2 tbspns

Remove the air from the bag and close it tightly, then gently massage and mix the chicken, yoghurt and spice until all nicely covered.

Put the bag in the fridge and leave

When ready to go, on a medium heat, add the rapeseed oil to the frying pan

KEY TIMER add the onion and slowly cook it, not flash frying! 10 mins minimum but as long as you can go!

KEY Add the contents of the freezer bag, so the chicken strips and **all** of the yoghurt and spice mix and cook until the chicken starts to brown and is cooked through (use a meat thermometer if not sure but quickly cutting into one will tell you)

KEY TIMER Add the ginger, garlic, curry powder, garam masala and sliced peppers and continue to cook for another 5 minutes

Stir in the remainder of the yoghurt and add the stock, stirring until well combined

KEY TIMER Let it slowly simmer away for another 5-10 mins but not boil too vigorously

Just before service, add in the fresh coriander and mix in

Ready to serve as you wish

# Vegetable Creamy Curry

***Still Tastes Great!***

**Difficult rating:** ★★★☆☆
**Serves:** min 4
**Cooking time:** 20 mins
**Preparation time:** 15 mins
**Give Yourself Time:** 40 mins

## You Will Need

*Large deep frying pan*
*Knife*
*Chopping board*
*Large plastic or metal mixing spoon*
*Cup*
*Teaspoon*
*Tablespoon*

## Ingredients

- 1 white onion, peeled and chopped (a cup of frozen is fine too)
- 1 tspn chopped garlic
- 1 tspn chopped ginger
- 1 heaped tspn curry powder (your choice of heat)
- 1 heaped tspn garam masala
- 1 cup frozen sliced mixed peppers or ½ red and ½ yellow fresh sliced
- 4 tbspns plain natural yoghurt
- 250ml vegetable stock (from a cube ok)
- 2 tbspns rapeseed oil for frying
- ½ courgette cut into rounds
- 3 large tomatoes cut into ¼ s
- Tin of chickpeas, drained
- Handful of fresh spinach, or 2 blocks of frozen
- 1 small bag of mange tout
- Handful of fresh coriander torn into bits

## Method

On a medium heat, add the rapeseed oil to the frying pan

KEY TIMER add the onion and slowly cook it, not flash frying!  10 mins minimum but as long as you can go!

Add the chickpeas, tomatoes, courgette and mange tout and fry for a couple of minutes

KEY TIMER Add the ginger, garlic, curry powder, garam masala and sliced peppers and continue to cook for another 5 minutes

Stir in the yoghurt and add the stock, stirring until well combined

Add the spinach and stir through

KEY TIMER Let it slowly simmer away for another 5-10 mins but not boil too vigorously

You may need a little extra water if it is looking a bit dry

Just before serving add in the fresh coriander and mix in

Ready to serve as you wish

# Chicken Fajitas

*Everyone Loves Build Your Own Food!*

**Difficult rating:** ★★★½☆
**Serves:** 4
**Cooking time:** 10 mins
**Preparation time:** 15 mins
**Give Yourself Time:** 35 mins

## You Will Need

*Knife*
*Chopping board*
*Large deep frying pan*
*Large mixing bowl*
*Spatula*
*Baking tray*
*Teaspoon*
*Tablespoon*

## Ingredients

- 3 fresh chicken breasts cut into strips
- 1 white onion peeled and cut into half moons
- 1 yellow pepper cut into slices (must be fresh and frozen won't work)
- 1 red pepper cut into slices (must be fresh and frozen won't work)
- 1 tspn chopped garlic
- 1 tspn chopped ginger
- 1 tspn ground cumin
- Juice of ½ lemon, or a whole lime
- 1 tspn smoked paprika
- 1 tspn ground coriander
- 8 gluten free tortilla wraps
- 1 small tub crème freche or sour cream
- 1 small tub tomato salsa
- 1 small tub guacamole *(see recipe on page 130)*
- ½ iceberg lettuce cut into shreds
- Splash of water
- 2 tbspns rapeseed oil
- Bowl grated cheddar cheese

## Method

KEY pre heat the oven to 200C

In the mixing bowl, put together the coriander, cumin, garlic, ginger, smoked paprika, lemon or lime juice, a splash of water and mix well to combine

Add in the chicken strips, peppers and onion and mix well to ensure everything is coated in the mix (the longer you can leave this the better but it works if using straight away)

Heat the frying pan to a medium high level and add the contents of the bowl (the chicken mix). There is oil in here already so you don't need any more

KEY TIMER Fry for 5-6 minutes, until chicken is cooked through, moving sporadically. Test a bit of chicken if you don't have a thermometer, just to ensure no pink bits

Warm the tortillas in the oven as per the instructions on their packet (if no instructions just wrap them in foil and put in the oven on a tray for 2 minutes)

Have the guacamole, salsa, cheese, crème freche/sour cream in little bowls.

Put the chicken mix into a serving bowl and the tortilla wraps on a plate in the centre of the table with the above

Let everyone dig in and fill their tortillas as they see fit!

### Hints & Tips

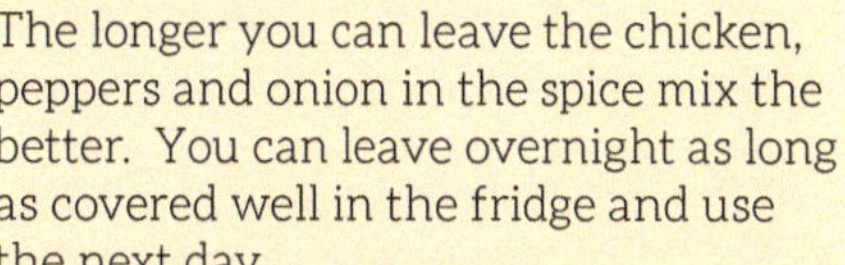

The longer you can leave the chicken, peppers and onion in the spice mix the better. You can leave overnight as long as covered well in the fridge and use the next day.

### Ways To Change

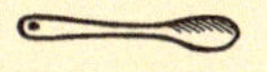

You can use turkey or pork strips for a change

Add chilli flakes or fresh chilli if you like it hot, but maybe have some chopped fresh chilli's in a separate bowl for people to add as they see fit

Have some cooked rice there as an additional topping to put inside the tortillas

Do it vegetarian by removing the chicken strips and adding more veg of your choice. Tender stem broccoli is lovely

# Rice Krispie Chicken Nuggets

*Simple, yet Cracking!*

**Difficult rating:** ★★★☆☆
**Serves:** 4-6
**Cooking time:** 15 mins
**Preparation time:** 15 mins
**Give Yourself Time:** 40 mins

### You Will Need

*Baking tray lined with foil*
*Small bowl*
*3 large flat plates*
*Knife*
*Chopping board*
*Fork / whisk*

### Ingredients

- 4 chicken breasts cut into nugget sized pieces (you can buy ready cubed chicken breast if having a bad one)
- 2 free range eggs
- Gluten free rice krispie snaps
- Gluten free plain flour
- Salt & pepper

### Method

KEY preheat the oven to 180C

Break the eggs into the bowl, add a pinch of salt and pepper then whisk to combine well

Arrange the 3 plates side by side and start from left to right (if right handed) or right to left (if left handed)

On the first plate tip on some gluten free plain flour, about a cm thick all over

On the middle plate, pour the egg mix onto it, making sure don't lose any

On the last plate, pour on the rice krispies, again about a cm thick

Take the chicken pieces a few at a time and place in the flour

Remove any excess flour before placing them in the eggs, rolling to coat all over

Allow any excess egg mix to drip off before placing into the rice krispies, again rolling to ensure completely covered

Put the nuggets onto the baking tray

Repeat until you have done all of your chicken pieces

KEY put the tray of nuggets into the fridge for a minimum of 10 mins to allow them to firm a little

A few minutes before ready to bake, remove the nuggets from the fridge to get to room temperature

KEY TIMER put into the oven for 15 minutes

Depending on how big your nuggets are you may need to adjust the timings. Use a meat thermometer to check or cut one open to be sure

Serve hot with home made chips or wedges *(see recipe on page 135)*
and salad *(see recipes on pages 99-102)*

### Hints & Tips

KEY use **one hand for the dry ingredient** dips and **one for the wet** – it saves a lot of gloop on your fingers and keeps the nuggets nice and even

### Ways To Change

Add some chilli powder to the flour and mix through for a spicy kick

Curry powder in the flour mix also adds extra flavour

# Chicken One Pot

*Make it, leave it, eat it!*

**Difficult rating:** ★★☆☆☆
**Serves:** 4
**Cooking time:** 60-70 mins
**Preparation time:** 20 mins
**Give Yourself Time:** 100 mins

## You Will Need

*Knife*
*Chopping board*
*Vegetable peeler*
*Casserole dish & lid (make sure it fits in your oven before you make this!)*
*Deep based large frying pan*
*Measuring jug*
*Teaspoon*
*Large metal spoon*
*Tablespoon*

## Ingredients

- 4 chicken breasts (whole)
- 12 new potatoes cut into ½'s
- 16 plumb or cherry tomatoes (whole)
- 1 white onion peeled and chopped (cup frozen also great)
- 1 tspn chopped garlic
- 1 tspn chopped ginger
- 1 litre vegetable stock (cube ok)
- 2 bay leaves
- 1 sprig fresh thyme (stalks and all)
- 2 carrots peeled and chopped into thumb nail size pieces
- 6 tender stem broccoli
- 4 tbspns rapeseed oil

### Hints & Tips

Make sure your casserole dish will fit into your oven before you start to fill it!

Be careful when taking the lid off the dish as the steam is lethal! A good facial but hot!

### Ways To Change

Add some chopped fresh chilli to the veg mix for some spice

Add mushrooms, but keep them chunky and fry with the onion mix

Chicken thighs are a great alternative, cheaper too

## Method

KEY preheat the oven to 180C

Add ½ the oil to the frying pan on a medium high heat

KEY Brown the chicken breasts on both sides, but you are **not looking to cook through here**

Set aside the chicken

KEY TIMER Add the rest of the oil to the pan and add the onion, garlic, ginger, carrots and tomatoes and fry for 2 mins

KEY TIMER Add the potatoes and continue to fry for another minute

Add half of the veg mix to the bottom of the casserole dish

Lay the chicken breasts on top

Add the remainder of the veg mix

Pour over the vegetable stock and add in the bay leaves and thyme stalks

KEY TIMER put the lid on and into the oven for 1 hour

KEY TIMER carefully remove the dish, take off the lid (and watch for the steam) and add in the broccoli stems

KEY TIMER Replace the lid and back into the oven for 10 mins

Serve with some gluten free bread to mop up that sauce

# Turkey Steak Pizzas

*Sounds a bit weird but, trust me! Healthy alternative*

**Difficult rating:** ★★★☆☆
**Serves:** 4
**Cooking time:** 30 mins
**Preparation time:** 20 mins
**Give Yourself Time:** 60 mins

**You Will Need**

*Knife*
*Chopping board*
*Baking tray*
*Teaspoon*
*Tablespoon*
*2 deep frying pans*
*Spatula*

**Hints & Tips** 

Serve as soon as they are ready

You can make the tomato pepper mix ahead and reheat when ready

**Ways To Change** 

Add some chilli to the tomato and pepper mix for a bit of kick

Serve with rice and/or salad

Or garlic bread if the kids beg!

## Ingredients

- 4–6 × turkey steaks
- ½ punnet of cherry tomatoes – cut into quarters
- Half a white onion chopped
- 1 tbspn gluten free tomato ketchup
- 1 × tspn of chopped garlic
- 1 × mozzarella ball
- 1 × tspn of chopped ginger
- 1 × tspn dried basil – or 5-6 fresh leaves ripped up
- 2 cups of frozen mixed peppers (or raw)
- Salt & pepper
- 3-4 × rashers of smoky bacon cut into small chunks
- Rapeseed oil
- 3 × tbspns passata

## Method

KEY Pre heat the oven to 220c

KEY TIMER In a frying pan, heat the rapeseed oil and fry the bacon and onion for 10 mins until cooked through

KEY TIMER Add the peppers, garlic and ginger and continue to fry for 5 mins

KEY TIMER Add all of the chopped tomatoes, the passata, basil and the ketchup and cook on a low heat for 10 mins

Meanwhile, in a separate pan or griddle pan, fry the turkey steaks quickly on each side until brown but not cooked through. Set aside

On a baking tray, lay the turkey steaks flat

Spoon on the vegetable mix to each steak as if it is a pizza but slightly more piled up

Tear the mozzarella ball into chunks and place 2 on each pizza

KEY TIMER Put into the hot oven for 10 mins until cheese gone golden brown

Serve

# Spaghetti Carbonara

*My girls love this one, slurping up the spaghetti!*

**Difficult rating:** ★★★☆☆
**Serves:** 4-6
**Cooking time:** 20 mins
**Preparation time:** 15 mins
**Give Yourself Time:** 45 mins

**You Will Need**

*Knife*
*Chopping board*
*Measuring jug*
*Whisk*
*Teaspoon*
*Large saucepan*
*Spatula*
*Deep based frying pam*
*Tongues*
*Tablespoon*

## Ingredients

- 100g per person of gluten free spaghetti
- 1 tsp mixed herbs / Italian herbs
- ½ cup cream (single)
- 1 tsp crushed garlic
- 1 packet unsmoked bacon cut into pieces
- Salt & pepper
- 2 eggs lightly beaten (free range if can)
- 2 tbspns rapeseed oil
- 1 small white onion diced (or cup frozen good)
- 1 cup grated cheese

## Method

KEY TIMER Cook the spaghetti in a large pan of salted boiling water according to the instructions on the packet

Whilst it is cooking, fry the bacon and onion in a large frying pan in some rapeseed oil

KEY TIMER When starting to colour, add the garlic and continue to cook for a further 2-3 mins then set aside

KEY Once the spaghetti is cooked, drain it but **retain a half a cup of the cooking water**

Return the pan with the bacon mix to the heat

When starting to fizz, add the cooking water from the pasta, the cream and the cheese and heat through

Stir in the spaghetti and the mixed herbs

Once a good heat, pour in the eggs, salt and pepper and stir quickly to ensure the eggs coat all of the pasta and are cooked

Serve with gluten free garlic bread and some parmesan cheese

### Hints & Tips

Keeping back that cooking water is crucial to getting a silky sauce

Give yourself time to cook the onions and bacon mix properly, nothing worse than floppy bacon!

### Ways To Change

You can add a nice white wine to the onion and bacon mix if you like for added flavour, just watch it if for the younger ones!

You can add chicken to this if you like, or even salmon

Try different types of gluten free pasta, so penne (tubes) fusilli (spirals) conchiglie (shells) or tagliatelle (thicker spaghetti)

Try brown rice pasta or pea pasta (green, yes it exists) or even lentil pasta (orange) for different colours, flavours and textures – makes one dish go in so many different ways

# Toad in the Hole

*Comfort Food!*

**Difficult rating:** ★★½☆☆
**Serves:** 4
**Cooking time:** 35 mins
**Preparation time:** 5* mins
**Give Yourself Time:** 50* mins
**Add time for making the Yorkshire pudding* *(see recipe on page 143)*

### You Will Need

*Medium sized square oven dish*
*Large deep frying pan*
*Yorkshire pudding mix* *(see recipe on page 143)*
*Tongues*
*Tablespoon*
*Pouring jug (for batter)*

### Ingredients

- 8 gluten free sausages of your choice
- Yorkshire pudding batter mix *(see recipe on page 143)*
- Tablespoon rapeseed oil for frying

### Method

KEY preheat the oven to 200C

Make up the Yorkshire pudding batter and let it rest *(as per recipe on 143)*

Add the oil to the frying pan and on a medium heat brown the sausages but don't overcook at this stage

KEY Carefully, using the tongues, transfer the sausages to the cooking dish and put in evenly across the bottom, **and add the hot oil from the pan**

Pour over the Yorkshire pudding batter

KEY TIMER put into the oven for 25-30 mins

KEY Check after 25 mins if needs more time, usually the centre is the place to check if is still needing more cooking

Remove and serve in the dish just with garden peas or baked beans, even beef gravy is lovely poured over!

### Hints & Tips

Adding the hot oil that the sausages were cooked in, to the cooking dish gives the Yorkshire pudding batter something to fire off so always pour it in

Yorkies are notoriously fickle, so one day 25 mins is fine, the next it is 30 so please do check

### Ways To Change

Have some slow cooked onions ready to go with the dish, adds a lovely sweetness

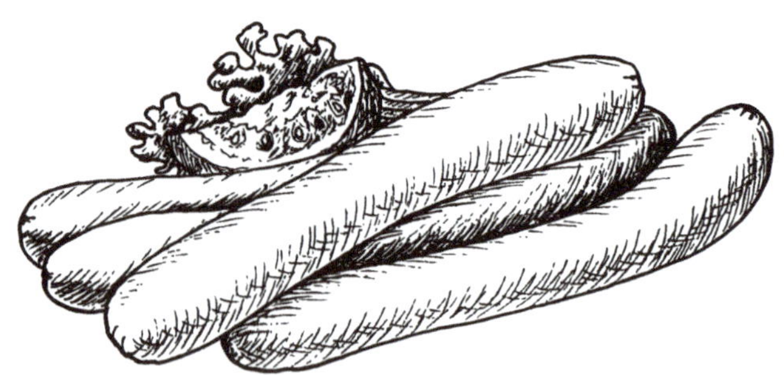

*Great on a cold day.........or any day!*

**Difficult rating:** ★★★☆☆
**Serves:** 4
**Cooking time:** 70 mins
**Preparation time:** 20 mins
**Give Yourself Time:** 105 mins

## You Will Need

*Large casserole dish with lid (please check it fits in the oven before you fill it!)*
*Large deep frying pan*
*Measuring jug*
*Teaspoon*
*Tablespoon*
*Vegetable peeler*
*Tongues*
*Large mixing spoon*
Cup

## Ingredients

- 4 pork steaks / chops
- 2 carrots peeled and chopped into thumb nail size pieces
- 1 white onion peeled and roughly chopped (1 cup of frozen is good)
- 1 tbspn chopped ginger
- 1 tspn chopped garlic
- ½ swede / turnip peeled and chopped into same size chunks as carrots
- 12 new potatoes cut into ½'s
- 1 litre vegetable stock (cube great)
- 2 bay laves
- 4 tbspns rapeseed oil

## Hints & Tips

If there is any of the veg mix left over, don't throw it away! It makes a lovely soup as is or you can blitz it up for a smoother soup

Always check you casserole dish, with the lid on, will fit in your oven **before** you add the food inside!

## Ways To Change 

Add some chopped fresh chilli to the veg mix for some spice

Add mushrooms, but keep them chunky and fry with the onion mix

## Method

KEY preheat the oven to 180C

Add half the oil to the frying pan

KEY Under a medium high heat add the pork steaks and quickly colour on both sides – **not looking to cook through here just colour**

Set aside the pork steaks

KEY TIMER Add the remainder of the oil to the same frying pan and add the garlic, onion, ginger, carrot and swede and brown quickly for 2 mins

Add the potatoes to the frying pan and stir well then turn off the heat

In the casserole dish, add half of the veg mix

Then lay the pork steaks on top

Add the remainder of the veg mix

Pour over the veg stock

Add the bay leaves

KEY TIMER Put the lid on and into the oven for 1 hour

Serve with some gluten free bread to help the mop up

# Sausage Casserole

*You Beauty!*

**Difficult rating:** ★★★☆☆
**Serves:** 4
**Cooking time:** 60-70 mins
**Preparation time:** 20 mins
**Give Yourself Time:** 100 mins

## You Will Need

*Knife*
*Chopping board*
*Measuring jug*
*Casserole dish and lid (make sure fits into oven before filling)*
*Teaspoon*
*Deep based frying pan*
*Large mixing spoon*
*Vegetable peeler*
*Tablespoon*
*Tongues*
*Cup*

## Ingredients

- 8 gluten free sausages of your choice
- 1 white onion peeled and chopped (1 cup of frozen good)
- 12 new potatoes cut into ½'s
- 1 litre vegetable stock (cube good)
- 1 tspn chopped garlic
- 1 tspn chopped ginger
- 2 bay leaves
- 2 carrots peeled and chopped into bitesize pieces
- 2 parsnips peeled and cut into bite size pieces
- 4 tbspns rapeseed oil for frying

### Hints & Tips

Any left-over vegetable mix do not throw away! It makes a fantastic soup, either chunky as is or whizzed up smooth.

Make sure you check the casserole dish with the lid on will fit in the oven before you fill it up!

### Ways To Change

Add some French mustard to the stock before pouring in, lovely

Add a can of tomatoes before pouring over the stock for a tangy extra

## Method

KEY preheat the oven to 180C

KEY Add ½ the oil to the frying pan and under a medium heat add the sausages and brown quickly (**not looking to cook through, just colour**)

Remove the sausages from the pan and set aside

KEY TIMER Using the same frying pan, add the rest of the oil and add the onion, garlic, ginger, carrots and parsnips and fry for 2 minutes

KEY TIMER add the potatoes to the frying pan and cook for a further 2 minutes

Add half of the vegetable mix to the bottom of the casserole dish

Lay the sausages on top

Add the remainder of the vegetable mix

Pour over the stock and add the bay leaves

KEY TIMER put the lid on and put in the oven for 1 hour

Serve with some gluten free bread to soak up the scrumminess

# Vegetable Stuffed Peppers

*No, Not The '70's, great!*

**Difficult rating:** ★★★½☆
**Serves:** 4
**Cooking time:** 35-40 mins
**Preparation time:** 15 mins
**Give Yourself Time:** 60 mins

## You Will Need

*Knife*
*Chopping board*
*Large deep frying pan*
*Spatula*
*Mixing spoon*
*Medium saucepan*
*Baking tray or dish*
*Blitzer*
*Teaspoon*
*Tablespoon*

## Ingredients

- 4 bell peppers (mix up the colours)
- 200g quinoa or rice
- 100g gluten free bread crumbs (break up and then blitz in blender to make fine crumbs)
- 1 tspn chopped garlic
- 1 tspn chopped ginger
- 1 whole white onion peeled and chopped (a cup of frozen good)
- ½ tspn dried chilli flakes
- 8 plum tomatoes chopped into small pieces
- 1 tspn gluten free soy sauce or gf Worcester sauce if prefer
- ½ courgette chopped into small dices
- 2 mozzarella balls sliced into rounds
- Salt and pepper
- 3 tbspns rapeseed oil for frying

## Method

KEY preheat the oven to 200C

KEY TIMER cook the quinoa or rice to the packet instructions

In the frying pan, add the oil and bring to medium high heat

KEY TIMER Add the onion, garlic, ginger, breadcrumbs and chilli and fry until soft, 2 mins

Add the soy/worcester sauce and continue to cook for a minute more

Add the quinoa / rice to the pan and mix thoroughly

Carefully cut the top off the peppers and set aside the tops

Turn the peppers upside down and gently bang then to get the seeds out

Turn back the right way up and arrange them on the baking try or dish

If the peppers won't stand up on their own, use some scrumpled up foil around the base to hold it up

KEY Using a spoon, carefully fill each pepper **halfway up** with the mix

Add a slice of mozzarella into each pepper on top of the mix

KEY Add more of the mix on top to just below the top of each pepper, **keeping some back for the topping**

Add another circle of mozzarella and finally top with the remaining mixture

Take the tops of the peppers you removed and add them back on top of the peppers. I like to use different colours rather than like on like!

KEY TIMER put into the oven for 20-25 mins

Serve with salad and a tub of crème freche or sour cream

You can eat the pepper too of course!

### Hints & Tips

Scrumpled up tin foil is a great way to prop things up if they are wobbling a bit

### Ways To Change

Use different types of rice or quinoa

Cook the rice / quinoa in some stock to add more flavour

# Mince Stuffed Peppers

Take the recipe for the vegetable peppers but change as follows:

Add 150g minced beef, pork or turkey and fry with the onion mix until brown

- ½ the number of tomatoes used in the vegetable recipe
- Reduce the quinoa / rice to 150g

Everything else is the same

# Egg Fried Rice

*It's worth it for the flavours and a lovely family meal*

**Difficult rating:** ★★★☆☆
**Serves:** 4-6
**Cooking time:** 15 mins
**Preparation time:** 10 mins
**Give Yourself Time:** 35 mins

### You Will Need

*Medium sauce pan*
*Small bowl*
*Whisk*
*Spatula*
*Large deep frying pan*
*Cup*
*Tablespoon*
*Teaspoon*

### Ingredients

- 1 tbspn of rapeseed oil
- 1 cup of frozen peas
- 1 small onion diced
- 2 free range eggs lightly beaten
- 1 tspn chopped garlic
- 2 tbspns gluten free soy sauce
- 1 tspn chopped ginger
- Salt and pepper
- 1 family packet of microwaveable rice (or cook equiv of loose if want)
- 1 cup of frozen sweetcorn

### Method

Heat the oil in a wok or large frying pan over a high heat

KEY TIMER Add the onion and lower the heat slightly to cook for 10 mins

KEY TIMER Add the garlic and ginger and fry for a further 2-3 mins

KEY TIMER Cook the rice as per the packet instructions and allow to cool a little

KEY TIMER Add the sweetcorn and peas to the onion mix and stir fry for a further 2-3 mins

Add the cooked rice and separate in the mixture (if adding separately cooked rice, allow to cool a little before adding)

Add the soy sauce and salt and pepper (careful with the salt as soy sauce already salty)

Create a well in the middle of the rice in the pan

Pour in the egg and stir slowly until it starts to cook

As it cooks but remains liquidy, gradually widen the stirring circle to combine the egg into the rice

Serve immediately as the egg will continue to cook so you want it to stay light and fluffy

### Hints & Tips

Have the rice pre-cooked and cooled ahead of the game as the cooler the rice the better the stir fry

Be careful of the soy sauce and salt combination as both very salty

### Ways To Change

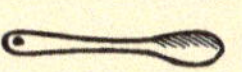

Add mange tout to the onion mixture for added crunch

Add tender stemmed broccoli at same time for colour and flavour

Add cooked chicken or the meat/fish of your choice with the rice as you get more confident with it

Add pak choi, cut into ¼ s and push well into the frying pan with the onion mix, before the rice goes in, and put the lid on to steam it for a couple of minutes, then add the rice

# Pepper filled Egg Fried Rice

*It's worth it for the flavours and a lovely family meal*

**Difficult rating:** ★★★☆☆
**Serves:** 4-6
**Cooking time:** 15 mins
**Preparation time:** 10 mins

**Give Yourself Time:** 35 mins

### You Will Need

*Medium sauce pan*
*Small bowl*
*Whisk*
*Spatula*
*Large deep frying pan*
*Cup*
*Tablespoon*
*Teaspoon*
*Baking tray or dish*

### Ingredients

- 1 tbspn of rapeseed oil
- 1 cup of frozen peas
- 1 small onion diced
- 2 free range eggs lightly beaten
- 1 tspn chopped garlic
- 2 tbspns gluten free soy sauce
- 1 tspn chopped ginger
- Salt and pepper
- 1 family packet of microwaveable rice (or cook equiv of loose if want)
- 4 bell peppers mixed colour
- 1 cup of frozen sweetcorn

### Method

KEY preheat the oven to 200C

Heat the oil in a wok or large frying pan over a high heat

KEY TIMER Add the onion and lower the heat slightly to cook for 10 mins

KEY TIMER Add the garlic and ginger and fry for a further 2-3 mins

KEY TIMER Cook the rice as per the packet instructions and allow to cool a little

KEY TIMER Add the sweetcorn and peas to the onion mix and stir fry for a further 2-3 mins

Add the cooked rice and separate in the mixture (if adding separately cooked rice, allow to cool a little before adding)

Add the soy sauce and salt and pepper (careful with the salt as soy sauce already salty)

Create a well in the middle of the rice in the pan

Pour in the egg and stir slowly until it starts to cook

As it cooks but remains liquidy, gradually widen the stirring circle to combine the egg into the rice

Cut the top off the peppers and set aside the lids

Turn the peppers upside down and gently bang to release the seeds

Turn the right way up and arrange in the baking tray or dish, using scrumpled up tin foil around the base if unsteady

Fill the peppers with the egg fried rice mix

Put the 'lids' back on in any order you like

KEY TIMER cook in the oven for 20-25 mins

Serve and enjoy

### Hints & Tips

Have the rice pre-cooked and cooled ahead of the game as the cooler the rice the better the stir fry

Be careful of the soy sauce and salt combination as both very salty

### Ways To Change

Add some sliced mozzarella cheese making layers of rice and cheese within the peppers

# Chicken Egg Fried Rice

*It's worth it for the flavours and a lovely family meal*

**Difficult rating:** ★★★☆☆
**Serves:** 4-6
**Cooking time:** 15 mins
**Preparation time:** 10 mins

**Give Yourself Time:** 35 mins

## You Will Need

*Medium sauce pan*
*Small bowl*
*Whisk*
*Spatula*
*Large deep frying pan*
*Cup*
*Tablespoon*
*Teaspoon*

## Ingredients

- 1 tbspn of rapeseed oil
- 1 cup of frozen peas
- 1 small onion diced
- 2 free range eggs lightly beaten
- 1 tspn chopped garlic
- 2 tbspns gluten free soy sauce
- 1 tspn chopped ginger
- Salt and pepper
- 1 family packet of microwaveable rice (or cook equiv of loose if want)
- 2-3 chicken breasts cut into strips (or ready cut fillets)
- 1 cup of frozen sweetcorn

### Hints & Tips

Have the rice pre-cooked and cooled ahead of the game as the cooler the rice the better the stir fry

Be careful of the soy sauce and salt combination as both very salty

### Ways To Change

Add mange tout to the onion mixture for added crunch

Add tender stemmed broccoli at same time for colour and flavour

Add pak choi, cut into ¼ s and push well into the frying pan with the chicken and onion mix, before the rice goes in, and put the lid on to steam it for a couple of minutes, then add the rice

## Method

Heat the oil in a wok or large frying pan over a high heat

KEY TIMER Add the onion and lower the heat slightly to cook for 10 mins

KEY TIMER Add the chicken, garlic and ginger and fry for a further 2-3 mins

KEY TIMER Cook the rice as per the packet instructions and allow to cool a little

KEY TIMER Add the sweetcorn and peas to the onion mix and stir fry for a further 2-3 mins

Add the cooked rice and separate in the mixture (if adding separately cooked rice, allow to cool a little before adding)

Add the soy sauce and salt and pepper (careful with the salt as soy sauce already salty)

Create a well in the middle of the rice in the pan

Pour in the egg and stir slowly until it starts to cook

As it cooks but remains liquidy, gradually widen the stirring circle to combine the egg into the rice

Serve immediately as the egg will continue to cook so you want it to stay light and fluffy

# The Basic One

*Like a curry or Bolognese – so versatile!*

**Difficult rating:** ★★★☆☆
**Serves:** 4-6
**Cooking time:** 6-10 mins
**Preparation time:** 15 mins
**Give Yourself Time:** 30 mins

### You Will Need

*Knife*
*Chopping board*
*Wok or deep wide frying pan with lid*
*Spatula*
*Tongues*
*Teaspoon*
*Tablespoon*
*Large mixing spoon*
*Cup*
*Vegetable peeler*

### Ingredients

- 1 tspn chopped garlic
- 1 tspn chopped ginger
- 1 white onion peeled and chopped into small pieces (cup frozen great also)
- 1 cup bean sprouts
- 1 tspn Chinese 5 spice
- 2 tbspns gluten free soy sauce
- 1 carrot peeled and cut into thin strips about 2 inches long each
- 1 cup mange tout sliced into 3 long ways (a small packet)
- 1 pak choi cut into ¼ s
- Salt and pepper
- Splash of water
- 3 tbspns rapeseed oil for frying

### Hints & Tips

Keep everything moving so it can't stick and everything cooks evenly

### Ways To Change

Add chicken strips or pork strips or beef strips and cook with the onions at stage 1

### Method

In the wok / frying pan, heat all of the oil to a high heat

KEY TIMER Add the onion, garlic, ginger and carrots and fry, keeping moving, for 3 minutes

KEY TIMER add the bean sprouts, mange tout strips and the 5 spice and fry for a further 2 minutes, keeping it moving

Add the pak choi, soy sauce, salt, pepper and splash of water

Put the lid on and give it all a shake

KEY TIMER leave for 2 minutes

Remove lid, quick stir and ready to go

# Stir Fries – Noodles

*Great Fun With Chop Sticks*

**Difficult rating:** ★★★☆☆
**Serves:** 4-6
**Cooking time:** 6-10 mins
**Preparation time:** 15 mins
**Give Yourself Time:** 30 mins

**You Will Need**

*Knife*
*Chopping board*
*Wok or deep wide frying pan with lid*
*Spatula*
*Tongues*
*Teaspoon*
*Tablespoon*
*Large mixing spoon*
*Cup*
*Vegetable peeler*

**Hints & Tips**

Keep everything moving so it can't stick and everything cooks evenly

**Ways To Change**

Add chicken strips or pork strips or beef strips and cook with the onions at stage 1

**Ingredients**

- 1 tspn chopped garlic
- 1 tspn chopped ginger
- 1 white onion peeled and chopped into small pieces (cup frozen great also)
- 1 cup bean sprouts
- 1 tspn Chinese 5 spice
- 2 tbspns gluten free soy sauce
- 1 carrot peeled and cut into thin strips about 2 inches long each
- 1 cup mange tout sliced into 3 long ways (a small packet)
- 1 pak choi cut into ¼ s
- Salt and pepper
- Splash of water
- 3 tbspns rapeseed oil for frying
- 2 small packets of gluten free ready made rice noodles

**Method**

In the wok / frying pan, heat all of the oil to a high heat

KEY TIMER Add the onion, garlic, ginger and carrots and fry, keeping moving, for 3 minutes

KEY TIMER add the bean sprouts, mange tout strips and the 5 spice and fry for a further 2 minutes, keeping it moving

Add the noodles, pak choi, soy sauce, salt, pepper and splash of water and combine well

Put the lid on and give it all a shake

KEY TIMER leave for 2 minutes

Remove lid, quick stir and ready to go

# Stir Fries – The Spicy One

*Check who likes heat first!*

**Difficult rating:** ★★★☆☆
**Serves:** 4-6
**Cooking time:** 6-10 mins
**Preparation time:** 15 mins
**Give Yourself Time:** 30 mins

**You Will Need**

*Knife*
*Chopping board*
*Wok or deep wide frying pan with lid*
*Spatula*
*Tongues*
*Teaspoon*
*Tablespoon*
*Large mixing spoon*
*Cup*
*Vegetable peeler*

## Ingredients

- 1 tspn chopped garlic
- 1 tspn chopped ginger
- 1 white onion peeled and chopped into small pieces (cup frozen great also)
- 1 cup bean sprouts
- 1 tspn Chinese 5 spice
- 2 tbspns gluten free soy sauce
- 1 carrot peeled and cut into thin strips about 2 inches long each
- 1 cup mange tout sliced into 3 long ways (a small packet)
- 1 pak choi cut into ¼ s
- Salt and pepper
- Splash of water
- 3 tbspns rapeseed oil for frying
- 2 small packets of ready made gluten free rice noodles (optional)
- 2 tspns dried chilli flakes

### Hints & Tips

Keep everything moving so it can't stick and everything cooks evenly

### Ways To Change

Add chicken strips or pork strips or beef strips and cook with the onions at stage 1

## Method

In the wok / frying pan, heat all of the oil to a high heat

KEY TIMER Add the onion, garlic, ginger, chilli flakes and carrots and fry, keeping moving, for 3 minutes

KEY TIMER add the bean sprouts, mange tout strips and the 5 spice and fry for a further 2 minutes, keeping it moving

Add the noodles (optional), pak choi, soy sauce, salt, pepper and splash of water and combine well

Put the lid on and give it all a shake

KEY TIMER leave for 2 minutes

Remove lid, quick stir and ready to go

# Stir Fries – With Rice

*All in one!*

**Difficult rating:** ★★★☆☆
**Serves:** 4-6
**Cooking time:** 6-10 mins
**Preparation time:** 15 mins
**Give Yourself Time:** 30 mins

**You Will Need**

*Knife*
*Chopping board*
*Wok or deep wide frying pan with lid*
*Spatula*
*Tongues*
*Teaspoon*
*Tablespoon*
*Large mixing spoon*
*Cup*
*Vegetable peeler*

## Ingredients

- 1 tspn chopped garlic
- 1 tspn chopped ginger
- 1 white onion peeled and chopped into small pieces (cup frozen great also)
- 1 cup bean sprouts
- 1 tspn Chinese 5 spice
- 2 tbspns gluten free soy sauce
- 1 carrot peeled and cut into thin strips about 2 inches long each
- 1 cup mange tout sliced into 3 long ways (a small packet)
- 1 pak choi cut into ¼ s
- Salt and pepper
- Splash of water
- 3 tbspns rapeseed oil for frying
- Family sized packet of microwaveable rice or loose equivalent
- 2 tspns dried chilli flakes (optional)

### Hints & Tips

Keep everything moving so it can't stick and everything cooks evenly

### Ways To Change

Add chicken strips or pork strips or beef strips and cook with the onions at stage 1

## Method

Cook the rice as per the packet instructions

In the wok / frying pan, heat all of the oil to a high heat

KEY TIMER Add the onion, garlic, ginger, chilli flakes (optional) and carrots and fry, keeping moving, for 3 minutes

KEY TIMER add the bean sprouts, mange tout strips, rice and the 5 spice and fry for a further 2 minutes, keeping it moving

Add the pak choi, soy sauce, salt, pepper and splash of water and combine well

Put the lid on and give it all a shake

KEY TIMER leave for 2 minutes

Remove lid, quick stir and ready to go

# Stir Fries – Go East

*Fragrant!*

**Difficult rating:** ★★★☆☆
**Serves:** 4-6
**Cooking time:** 6-10 mins
**Preparation time:** 15 mins
**Give Yourself Time:** 30 mins

### You Will Need

*Knife*
*Chopping board*
*Wok or deep wide frying pan with lid*
*Spatula*
*Tongues*
*Teaspoon*
*Tablespoon*
*Large mixing spoon*
*Cup*
*Vegetable peeler*

### Ingredients

- 1 tspn chopped garlic
- 1 ½ tspns chopped ginger
- 1 white onion peeled and chopped into small pieces (cup frozen great also)
- 1 cup bean sprouts
- 1 tspn Chinese 5 spice
- 2 tbspns gluten free soy sauce
- 1 carrot peeled and cut into thin strips about 2 inches long each
- 1 cup mange tout sliced into 3 long ways (a small packet)
- 1 pak choi cut into ¼ s
- Salt and pepper
- Splash of water
- 3 tbspns rapeseed oil for frying
- 1 star Anise
- 1 tspn lemon grass paste
- ½ can water chestnuts drained

### Hints & Tips

Keep everything moving so it can't stick and everything cooks evenly

Remove the star anise before serving, not good to eat whole!

### Ways To Change

Add chicken strips or pork strips or beef strips and cook with the onions at stage 1

Add the gluten free rice noodles

Add the rice

Extra gluten free soy sauce is lovely dribbled on top when serving

### Method

Cook the rice as per the packet instructions

In the wok / frying pan, heat all of the oil to a high heat

KEY TIMER Add the onion, garlic, ginger, chilli flakes (optional) and carrots and fry, keeping moving, for 3 minutes

KEY TIMER add the star anise, lemon grass paste, water chestnuts, bean sprouts, mange tout strips, rice and the 5 spice and fry for a further 2 minutes, keeping it moving

Add the pak choi, soy sauce, salt, pepper and splash of water and combine well

Put the lid on and give it all a shake

KEY TIMER leave for 2 minutes

Remove lid, quick stir and ready to go

# Pizza Dough

*It's great fun and you feel a little Italian!*

**Difficult rating:** ★★★☆☆
**Serves:** 4-6
**Cooking time:** 15 mins
**Preparation time:** 20 mins
**Give Yourself Time:** 40 mins

### You Will Need

*Large mixing bowl*
*2 baking trays*
*Teaspoon*
*Tablespoon*
*Measuring jug*
*Weighing scales*
*Large metal spoon*

### Ingredients

- 400g gluten free bread flour
- 1 heaped tspn xanthum gum
- 1 tspn salt
- 2 tspns gluten free baking powder
- 5 tbspns rapeseed oil
- 1 tbspn caster sugar
- 250ml warm water

### Hints & Tips

Make the dough ahead and keep it in the fridge in a bowl with cling film over the top and it will be fine for a day

### Ways To Change

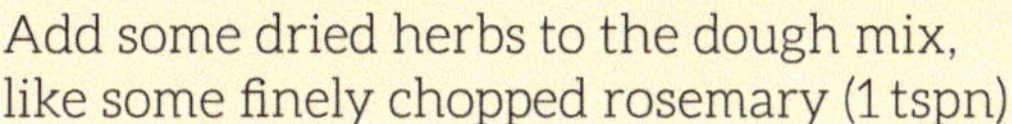

Add some dried herbs to the dough mix, like some finely chopped rosemary (1 tspn)

### Method

KEY preheat the oven to 200C

In the bowl, add the flour, sugar, baking powder, salt and xanthum gum and mix well

Make a well in the centre of the flour mix

Pour in the water and oil

Mix it together well using your hands to form a thick dough

This can be different each time so if you need a little more warm water, add 10-20ml as required

When you are ready to make a pizza

Get the 2 baking trays and lightly flour each with a scattering of gluten free flour (plain fine)

Split the dough into 2 equal parts

Push and pull the dough on each baking sheet to stretch it out as evenly as you can and to the thickness of pizza you like. For me, thin and crispy is the best so really pull it out

It doesn't matter what shape you end up with, that's the rustic look!

Add the pizza sauce *(see recipe on page 92)* in a thin layer, making sure to leave a 1cm gap around the edges so the crust can crisp up

Add the toppings of your choice *(see recipe on page 93)*

Bake in the oven for 10 mins and the sides are crisp

Remove, cut and serve!

# Pizza Tomato Sauce Topping

*Once you've made this you won't go back!*

**Difficult rating:** ★★☆☆☆
**Serves:** 4-6
**Cooking time:** 20 mins
**Preparation time:** 10 mins
**Give Yourself Time:** 35 mins

**You Will Need**

*Large deep frying pan*
*Spatula*
*Cup*
*Knife*
*Chopping board*
*Teaspoon*
*Tablespoon*

## Ingredients

- 1 × 400g can of chopped tomatoes
- 2 tbspns tomato puree
- 1 white onion peeled and chopped finely – cup frozen also good
- 1 tspn chopped garlic
- 304 fresh basil leaves ripped into pieces
- Pinch sugar
- 2 tbspns rapeseed oil

### Hints & Tips

Once cooled you can store the sauce in an airtight container in the fridge for up to 48 hours

If you really can't face making this, get a jar of passata with herbs in, which you can buy ready made, and use as the topping!

### Ways To Change

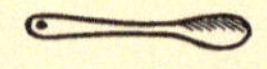

Add some chilli flakes for a kick

## Method

Add the oil to the frying pan on a medium heat

KEY TIMER Add the onion and garlic and cook for 2 minutes

Add the can of tomatoes and tomato puree and stir well to combine

KEY TIMER drop the heat to a simmer and cook for a further 15 minutes

Add the sugar and stir through

Add the ripped basil leaves, mix in and remove from the heat

The topping is ready to use but best if cooled and used cold on top of the dough

# Pizza All In

*Everyone loves pizza!*

**Difficult rating:** ★★☆☆☆
**Serves:** 4-6
**Cooking time:** 20 mins
**Preparation time:** 10 mins
**Give Yourself Time:** 35 mins

## You Will Need

*Baking trays (depending on how many making)*
*Metal spoon*
*Knife*
*Chopping board*

## Ingredients

- Pizza dough *(see recipe on page 91)*
- Your choice of toppings:
- Mozzarella, bacon strips, mixed peppers, ham, mushroom, chorizo, chilli, sausage etc
- Pizza tomato sauce topping *(see recipe on page 92)*

## Hints & Tips

Whatever you do, don't overload the pizza as it won't cook evenly and you will get either a soggy dough or burnt edges

If you really can't face making this, get a jar of passata with herbs in, which you can buy ready made, and use as the topping!

## Method

KEY preheat the oven to 200C

Lightly flour the baking trays

On each tray, pull and push the dough to the thickness and size you want

Spread the tomato topping over in a thin layer, leaving a 1cm edge around for the crust to crisp up

Add your favourite toppings, making sure not to overload

KEY TIMER bake in the oven for 10 minutes or until top golden brown and sides crisped up nicely

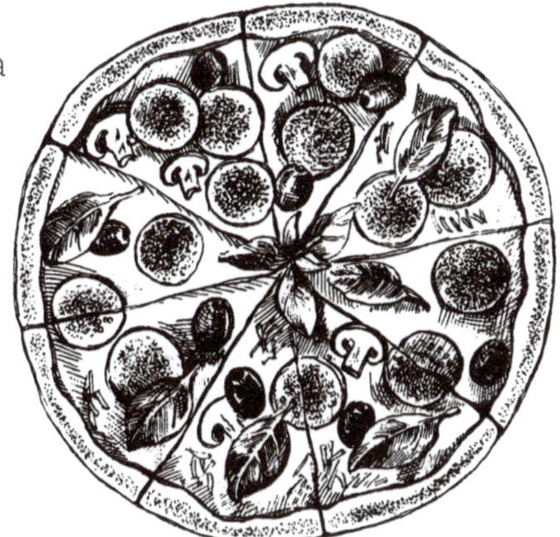

# Simple Omelette

*Once mastered – you can't beat them!*

**Difficult rating:** ★★½☆☆
**Serves:** 1
**Cooking time:** 5 mins
**Preparation time:** 5 mins
**Give Yourself Time:** 15 mins

**You Will Need**

*Measuring jug*
*Whisk or fork*
*Deep frying pan*
*Spatula*
*Teaspoon*

## Ingredients

- 3 free range eggs
- 1 tspn rapeseed oil
- 1 tsp butter
- Salt & pepper

## Method

Crack the eggs into the jug

Add a pinch of salt and pepper

Beat the eggs with the whisk or fork to combine

Put the butter and oil into the frying pan over a medium heat and let melt together

Tip the frying pan gently to get the oil mix around the bottom

Pour in the eggs and gently move the pan from side to side to ensure it is evenly covered

KEY TIMER **leave it for 20seconds** – don't mess with it

Free the edges around the outside of the pan with the spatula

Using the spatula, gently pull if through the middle of the egg mix creating a 1-2 inch gap

Tilt the pan to let the runny eggs go into the gap to fill it

Run the spatula around the edges again the ensure they are free from the side of the pan

Repeat the 2 above steps a couple of times more until the omelette is just set

Using your spatula, gently fold over one half of the omelette on top of the other – don't worry with some oozing, its ok!

KEY Leave for 30 seconds

Slide out of the pan to serve with a salad or chips

### Hints & Tips

If the eggs are cooking too fast and sticking, reduce the heat down

Be confident, and don't worry about ones going wrong, it will happen

### Ways To Change

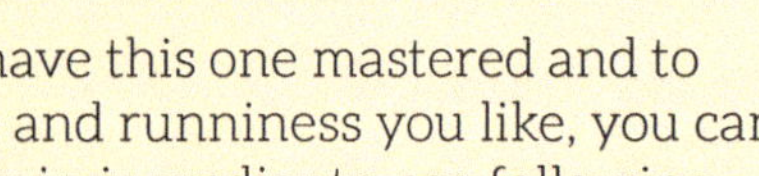

Once you have this one mastered and to the texture and runniness you like, you can start adding in ingredients, see following recipes

# Filled Omelette

*Just lovely comfort food!!*

**Difficult rating:** ★★½☆☆
**Serves:** 1
**Cooking time:** 5 mins
**Preparation time:** 6-7 mins

**Give Yourself Time:** 15 mins

## You Will Need

*Measuring jug*
*Whisk or fork*
*Deep frying pan*
*Spatula*
*Teaspoon*

## Ingredients

- 3 free range eggs
- 1 tspn rapeseed oil
- 1 tsp butter
- Salt & pepper

Your choice from:

- Grated cheese
- Chopped cooked bacon
- Sautéed mushrooms
- Sliced tomatoes
- Chilli flakes
- Flavoured cheeses
- Fresh herbs – coriander, basil etc
- Dried herbs

## Hints & Tips

If the eggs are cooking too fast and sticking, reduce the heat down

Be confident, and don't worry about ones going wrong, it will happen

Don't overfill as it will be a big fat mess

Put your filling onto the half of the omelette that you will be folding the other half onto, makes it whole lot easier!

## Method

Crack the eggs into the jug

Add a pinch of salt and pepper

Beat the eggs with the whisk or fork to combine

Put the butter and oil into the frying pan over a medium heat and let melt together

Tip the frying pan gently to get the oil mix around the bottom

Pour in the eggs and gently move the pan from side to side to ensure it is evenly covered

KEY TIMER **leave it for 20seconds** – don't mess with it

Free the edges around the outside of the pan with the spatula

Using the spatula, gently pull if through the middle of the egg mix creating a 1-2 inch gap

Tilt the pan to let the runny eggs go into the gap to fill it

Run the spatula around the edges again the ensure they are free from the side of the pan

Repeat the 2 above steps a couple of times more until the omelette is just set

Add in your choice of filling here but don't overload as it won't fold – add to the half you are going to fold onto, makes it easier!

Using your spatula, gently fold over one half of the omelette on top of the other – don't worry with some oozing, its ok!

KEY Leave for 30 seconds

Slide out of the pan to serve with a salad or chips

# Spanish Omelette

*Fancy and lovely!*

**Difficult rating:** ★★★☆☆
**Serves:** 4
**Cooking time:** 20 mins
**Preparation time:** 15 mins
**Give Yourself Time:** 45 mins

**You Will Need**

*Measuring jug*
*Whisk or fork*
*Deep wide frying pan with lid*
*Spatula*
*Teaspoon*
*Tablespoon*
*Large sauce pan*
*Colander / sieve*
*Vegetable peeler*
*Cup*

## Ingredients

- 6 free range eggs
- 500g maris piper potatoes peeled and cut into ½ cm slices
- 2 white onions peeled and chopped (2 cups frozen great)
- ½ tspn paprika
- ½ tspn smoked paprika
- Salt & pepper
- 4 tbspns rapeseed oil for frying

## Hints & Tips

Be gentle with the onions, not frying them but softening them slowly

Get the egg mix into every possible space you can as early as you can

Make sure your frying pan, without lid, will fit under your grill before you start!

Can be eaten hot or cold

Keeps well in the fridge once cold for a couple of days in an airtight container

## Method

KEY set your grill to hot and make sure there is space to put a frying pan under

KEY TIMER put the potatoes into a pan of salted boiling water and **cook for just 3minutes**

Drain and leave for later

KEY TIMER Put the oil into the frying pan and gently cook the onions under a medium/low heat for 10 minutes – not to brown

KEY TIMER add the cooled potatoes and continue to cook for a further 5-6 minutes

In the measuring jug, crack the eggs and add a pinch of salt and pepper and whisk well to combine

Add both paprikas to the onion and potato mix and cook for a minute and then pour over the egg mix

Try to get the egg mix into all the nooks and crannies in the pan by tipping back and forth gently

KEY TIMER put the lid on the frying pan and cook on a medium heat for 6-8 minutes

KEY TIMER Remove the lid and put the pan under the heated grill, keeping the handle away from the heat, until the top is golden brown and the eggs are cooked and set (max 5 mins)

Remove from the grill and allow to cool slightly

Using your spatula, gently free the edges from around the outsides of the pan and give the pan a little shake until it frees completely

Slide onto a serving plate, slice and enjoy!

# Salads

***Boring? Dull? Tasteless?.........NO!!!***

Look after your leaves, mix it up, keep them fresh, spice it up
Salad can be a main course as well as a side dish

## Basic Leaves To Try

**Little gem** – crunchy and adds texture

**Rocket** – peppery and fresh

**Spinach** – not just for Popeye! So versatile hot or cold

**Watercress** – spicy, so sparingly use!

**Iceberg** – basic but a great salad bulker for a budget

**Pea shoot salad** – tastes of ......peas!

## Great Fresh Herbs For Salad

**Mint** – fragrant and doesn't need a lot

**Basil** – perfumey and strong but so Italian tasting!

**Coriander** – savoury and delicious

**Chives** – great oniony kick

**TOP TIP** Use the stalks of fresh herbs too, chop them nice and fine and add as they contain loads of flavour and add a crunch

## Texture & Crunch

Salads often need more interest to keep you coming back, so added dimensions are always a good thing

**Croutons** so easy to make your own:

**Method**

KEY preheat the oven to 200C

Cut any sliced gluten free bread you have, crust 'n' all, into 2 cm squares

Put the bread onto a baking tray and drizzle over some rapeseed oil and sprinkle with a little salt

Gently mix them so that everything is nicely coated

KEY TIMER put into the oven for 10 mins
Remove carefully and let cool a little. You can use these warm on a salad, cold on a salad and they will keep in an airtight container for a couple of days

You can scatter some mixed herbs or chilli flakes on if you like too

## Seeds & Nuts

Please be careful if you have any allergies here

Seeds and nuts add flavour and texture to salads and also are very good for you (provided you don't have an allergy to any)

The following are my favourites

**Chia** – you can get these now in bags ready to sprinkle

**Pumpkin** – not just for the birds I promise

**Linseed** – oily and delicious

**Cashew** – of course

**Peanut** – if you can

**Sunflower** – wonderful flavour

As they are is fine, but you can also toast these to get some more flavour.

**Method**

All you need to do is put them into **a DRY frying pan**, **no oil**, and on a medium heat for a max of a couple of minutes and keep them moving.

You will smell when they are getting ready and take them out then

I like to make up a mix myself and have in airtight storage jars or containers ready to sprinkle!

You can make your own salads up that have no names, unless you name them yourself! Following though are some of my absolute favourites

# Greek Salad

*Tasty, fresh & wonderful!*

**Difficult rating:** ★★☆☆☆
**Serves:** 4-6 as side (double for main)
**Cooking time:** 0 mins
**Preparation time:** 20 mins
**Give Yourself Time:** 25 mins

## You Will Need

*Knife*
*Chopping board*
*Mixing bowl*
*Metal spoon*
*Serving bowl*
*Tablespoon*
*Teaspoon*

## Ingredients

- ¼ iceberg lettuce chopped roughly (not authentic but nice, leave out if want to)
- 1 packet feta cheese
- 6 large ripe tomatoes (room temperature and over ripe almost)
- 1 small red onion, peeled, halved and cut into half moons
- 1 cucumber, halved lengthways, seeds removed and cut into half moons
- 1 small tub olives
- 2 tspns dried oregano
- 4 tbspns olive oil
- Salt & pepper

## Hints & Tips

Keep everything reasonably chunky

To cut the cucumber, slice it along the length into half. Then with a metal spoon, scrape out the seeds of both halves. Then chop into half moons

## Ways To Change

Use different types of olives, flavours and colours for taste changes

## Method

Put the lettuce into the mixing bowl

Crumble in the feta in small irregular pieces

Cut the tomatoes into irregular chunks, the size of 1/4s but off centre, and add to the bowl

Add the onion, cucumber, olives, oregano, salt and pepper and the olive oil

Mix up with your hands gently trying not to break everything up but ensuring everything is nicely covered

Serve!

# Pepper Salad

*Colourful and wonderful!!*

**Difficult rating:** ★★★☆☆
**Serves:** 4-6 as side (double for main)
**Cooking time:** 0 mins
**Preparation time:** 25 mins
**Give Yourself Time:** 35 mins

## You Will Need

*Knife*
*Chopping board*
*Mixing bowl*
*Grater*
*Serving bowl*
*Tablespoon*
*Teaspoon*

## Ingredients

- Handful of spinach
- Handful of rocket
- Handful of watercress
- 1 red pepper sliced into strips
- 1 yellow pepper sliced into strips
- 2 carrots peeled
- 2 tbspns sesame seeds
- 4 tbspns garlic olive oil *(see recipe on page 133)*, (or olive oil a tspn chopped garlic)

## Hints & Tips

I find the easiest way to cut peppers is to stand them up on their end, then, holding the stalk, cut down one side of the pepper completely. Then just turn the pepper and cut the next side off until you have 4 off. Then you can easily slice them

## Ways To Change

Add some croutons or mixed seeds for more crunch if you want

## Method

Put the 3 leaves into the mixing bowl
Add the sliced peppers
Carefully grate the 2 carrots on the largest cheese side of the grater and add to the bowl
Add the sesame seeds, salt and pepper and garlic olive oil (or olive oil and garlic chopped)
Carefully mix well with your hands to ensure everything is well coated
Serve!

# Cold Pasta Salad

*Great way to use left over pasta!*

**Difficult rating:** ★★☆☆☆
**Serves:** 4
**Cooking time:** 0 mins
**Preparation time:** 20 mins
**Give Yourself Time:** 25 mins

## You Will Need

*Knife*
*Chopping board*
*Mixing bowl*
*Sauce pan (if cooking pasta fresh)*
*Serving bowl*
*Tablespoon*

## Ingredients

- 320g gluten free pasta (penne, fusilli, conchiglie etc)
- 1 tbspn pine nuts
- 1 tbspn cashew nuts
- 1 blood orange or large plain orange
- 2 tbspns olive oil
- ½ lemon zested and juiced
- Salt & pepper

## Method

Cook the pasta as per the instructions – or use cold from previous use

When it is cold, or luke warm, add to the bowl and add the pine nuts and cashew nuts

Add the olive oil, lemon zest, lemon juice and salt and pepper

Mix carefully with your hands or a metal spoon

Chop the blood orange into 1cm rounds

Carefully cut off the peel and pith

Cut into 2cm chunks or whatever size you prefer

Carefully add to the bowl and gently combine with your hands or a metal spoon

Serve

## Hints & Tips 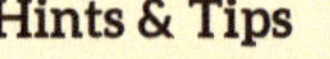

Just make sure everyone eating is ok with the nuts before making and serving

## Ways To Change 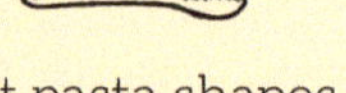

Try using different pasta shapes and flavours

Add some chilli flakes (1 tspn) for a bit of heat

Add some croutons or different seeds and nuts

Gently toast the nuts and seeds in a dry frying pan for 2 minutes max to release more nuttiness

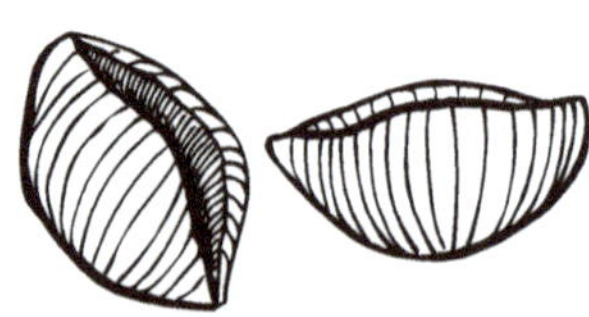
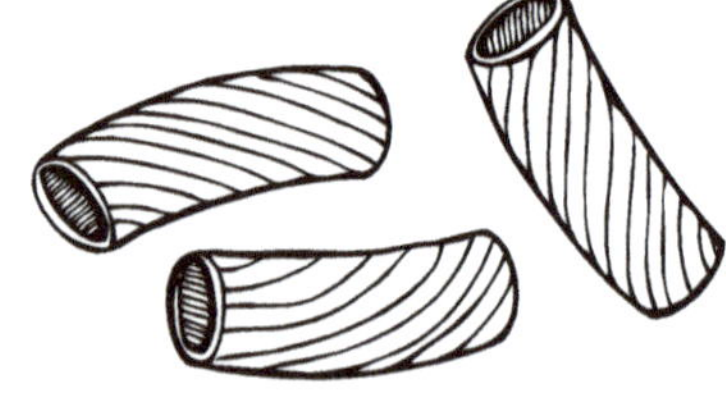

# Avocado & Egg Salad

*Weird but wonderful!*

**Difficult rating:** ★★☆☆☆
**Serves:** 4 as side (double for main)
**Cooking time:** 8 mins
**Preparation time:** 20 mins
**Give Yourself Time:** 35 mins

**You Will Need**

*Knife*
*Chopping board*
*Mixing bowl*
*Metal spoon*
*Serving bowl*
*Tablespoon*
*Teaspoon*
*Cup*
*Small saucepan*
*Colander / sieve*

## Ingredients

- 2 ripe avocados (press skin to check not too firm)
- 2 free range eggs
- 3 handfuls of salad leaves of your choice (I like spinach, watercress and pea shoot)
- 1 cup of cherry or plum tomatoes, quartered
- ½ cucumber sliced into rounds
- ½ cup croutons *(see recipe on page 97)*
- 2 tbspns olive oil
- Salt and pepper

**Hints & Tips**

Avocado can get messy so have a paper towel ready for your hands and board!

**Ways To Change**

Add some chilli flakes for some heat

A bit of mayonnaise also is lovely on this

## Method

KEY TIMER place the eggs into salted boiling water and cook for 8 minutes then remove and let cool in the shells

To cut the avocados, carefully run a knife round it lengthways, cutting right through to the stone. Twist the 2 halves away from each other and pull apart. In the side without the stone, carefully run a teaspoon around the inside of the skin until the half pops out.

To remove the stone from the other half - 2 ways. Either follow the same way as above to pop out the half and scoop out the stone, or, with the skin side down, carefully drop a sharp knife into the stone, twist it, and it should lift out

Chop the 2 halves into thin slices

Put the salad leaves into the bowl, add the avocado slices and combine gently.

Take the shells off the cooled eggs and cut into ¼'s

Add the eggs to the bowl

Add the tomato, cucumber, croutons, salt and pepper and olive oil

Gently combine and serve

# Hot to Cold Salads

*Salads aren't exclusively cold!*

**Difficult rating:** ★★☆☆☆

**Some ideas of hot that you can add to cold are:**

**Fried bacon strips** (smoky lovely as well) – and add the cooking oil as well as very tasty on leaves!

**Fried chorizo pieces** – again add the cooking oil for the lovely flavour and colour

**Hot croutons** *(see recipe on page 97)*

**Seeds and nuts** straight from a hot pan

**Warm chicken strips** – either left over from a Sunday lunch warmed up in the oven or new strips cooked especially

**Crushed new potatoes** – cook the potatoes as per the instructions in salted boiling water. Drain and gently squash them with the back of a fork to break them up. Pour over some olive oils, add salt and pepper, mix and add to any salad

**Boiled eggs** – shells removed and served when still warm and lovely!

The Sweet Stuff

# Filled Sweet Free Yorkshire Puddings

*Yes, that is what they were meant to be!*

**Difficult rating:** ★★★☆☆
**Serves:** 1-6 greedy kids
**Cooking time:** 30 mins
**Preparation time:** 10 mins
**Give Yourself Time:** 45 mins

**You Will Need**

*Measuring jug*
*Weighing scales*
*Whisk*
*Large mixing jug*
*Tablespoon*

## Ingredients

- 140g gluten free plain flour
- 2 tbsns soft brown sugar
- 50g corn flour
- A cup of grated chocolate
- 3 large free range eggs
- 175ml milk (whole or semi)
- Rapeseed oil
- Salt
- Ice cream of your choice

## Method

KEY Pre heat the oven to 200c

Sift the flour into a bowl (preferably a large pouring jug as easier later)

Add the sugar and teaspoon of salt and mix well

Crack the 3 eggs directly into the flour mix

Whisk well until combined and little or no flour showing

Add the milk little by little, whisking well each time to ensure no lumps

When all of the milk is combined set aside to rest for 15 mins minimum

Put a dribble of rapeseed oil into the wells of a 12 hole yorkie tin

KEY TIMER When ready to cook, put the tray into the oven for 5 mins for the oil to get hot

Very carefully remove the tin (oil is lethally hot) and pour in the batter mix to each well until level with the top of each well

KEY TIMER Put the tray back in the oven and cook for 25 mins

Carefully remove the yorkies from the tin

Allow to cool slightly then

Add a scoop of your favourite ice creams into the yorkie holes, a perfect fit!

Grate some of your favourite chocolate over the top

### Hints & Tips

Let the yorkie mix rest in the fridge when made for a good 30 mins to an hour and then re-whisk it again when ready to pour into the tin

### Ways To Change

Add some chopped mixed fruit instead of or under the ice cream - using frozen fruit is great as long as give time to defrost it a bit

Stewed fruit is lovely in the holes as well - see the recipe for fruit crumble to get the method of stewing fruit - even add the crumble topping to this for a real treat!

Add ice cream or custard

# Chocolate Brownies

*An absolute must!*

**Difficult rating:** ★★☆☆☆
**Serves:** 10-12
**Cooking time:** 40 mins
**Preparation time:** 20 mins
**Give Yourself Time:** 75 mins

**You Will Need**

*30 × 20 cm cake tin*
*Greaseproof paper for lining*
*Scissors*
*Small saucepan*
*2 mixing bowls (1 heatproof)*
*Spatula*
*Whisk (electric if have)*
*Teaspoon*
*Weighing scales*

## Ingredients

- 250g 70% min cocoa dark chocolate broken into small pieces
- 4 free range eggs
- 250g butter at room temperature
- 100g gluten free plain flour
- 300g golden caster sugar
- 60g cocoa powder
- 1 bag gluten free chocolate buttons
- ½ tspn vanilla extract

### Hints & Tips

To make lining a tin easier with paper, use a little dab of butter to act as a 'glue' between the paper and the tin, and it then sticks and doesn't flap about!

Don't overcook the brownies as dry ones aren't nice – so always go under than over if you can

### Ways To Change

They are just great as they are!

## Method

KEY preheat the oven to 180C

Line the cake tin with grease proof paper, using the scissors to cut to fit the base and around the sides

KEY Add water to the sauce pan no more than half the way up and bring to a **slow simmer - not boiling**

KEY put the heatproof bowl on top making sure it **doesn't touch the water underneath**

Add the butter and dark chocolate and slowly melt

KEY take it off the pan when it is just melted and leave to cool – **but not go cold and hard**

In a separate bowl, break in the eggs and add the sugar. Whisk until thick and creamy

Using a spatula, mix the chocolate mix into the egg mix

Add the vanilla extract, flour and cocoa powder and fold in to combine well

Mix in the chocolate buttons

KEY TIMER pour into the cake tin and into the oven for 30 mins

The top should give a bit when you gently push down

Let it cool a bit, cut and enjoy warm or cold

# Ready to go Yoghurt Fruit 'Ice Cream'

*Make, eat & enjoy*

**Difficult rating:** ★☆☆☆☆
**Serves:** 4
**Cooking time:** 0 mins
**Preparation time:** 10 mins
**Give Yourself Time:** 20 mins

**You Will Need**

*Blender*
*Spatula*
*Tablespoon*
*Measuring jug*
*Cup*
*Weighing scales*
*Teaspoon*

## Ingredients

- 4 tbspns sugar
- 150g Greek natural yoghurt
- ¼ tspn vanilla extract
- 4 cups frozen fruit (your choice of flavours!)

## Method

Put the frozen fruit into the blender, add the sugar, vanilla and half of the yoghurt

Give a quick blitz up to break up the frozen fruit

Add the rest of the yoghurt and whizz to the consistency you like – either small chunks of fruit or smooth

Serve it – now!

### Hints & Tips

You can put this into the freezer in an airtight container but it may go a little grainy – still wonderful though! The fruit has to be frozen – not fresh or defrosted

### Ways To Change

Use different frozen fruit

Use different flavoured Greek natural yoghurt to zing things up

# Eton Mess

*Naughty but nice!*

**Difficult rating:** ★☆☆☆☆
**Serves:** 4-6
**Cooking time:** 0 mins
**Preparation time:** 15 mins
**Give Yourself Time:** 25 mins

**You Will Need**

*2 × Mixing bowls (1 large)*
*Whisk*
*Knife*
*Chopping board*
*Measuring scales*
*Measuring jug*
*Tablespoon*

**Ingredients**

- 1 packet meringue nests
- 500g strawberries – topped and chopped roughly
- 450ml double cream
- 1 tbspn icing sugar

**Method**

In one mixing bowl, roughly break the meringues into pieces

In the second bowl, whisk the double cream and icing sugar together until just slightly stiff

Mix ¾'s of the strawberries into the cream

Whichever is the larger bowl, combine the meringues with the cream and strawberry mix carefully

Serve into bowls and top with the remaining strawberries

**Hints & Tips**

Not much to add really!

**Ways To Change**

Try different fruits – raspberries, mixed berries, tropical fruits

Add some chocolate buttons and sprinkles for the kids (all of us!)

Some fresh mint torn and added to the mix is lovely

# Pineapple Upside Down Cake

*For My Mum!*

**Difficult rating:** ★★★☆☆
**Serves:** 6-8
**Cooking time:** 35 mins
**Preparation time:** 25 mins
**Give Yourself Time:** 75 mins

### You Will Need

*Whisk*
*Large mixing bowl*
*Round cake tin or glass bowl*
*Wooden spoon*
*Can opener*
*Knife*
*Chopping board*
*Teaspoon*
*Tablespoon*
*Large flat plate*

### Ingredients

- 100g golden caster sugar
- 100g gluten free self-raising flour
- 100g butter, softened
- 1 tspn gluten free baking powder
- 2 free range eggs
- 1 tspn vanilla extract
- 1 tbspn golden syrup
- 1 can pineapple rings
- Small tub glace cherries
- Butter to coat the tin/bowl
- Sprinkle soft brown sugar

### Hints & Tips

If you are struggling with pain, get someone to help you with the flip part

Make sure you remember everything is built upside down to start with

### Ways To Change

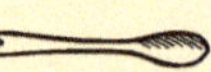

Serve with some ice cream, as it is or with custard as well

Don't change this, it is a classic!

### Method

KEY preheat the oven to 180C

Rub the butter for the coating into the base and sides of the bowl or tin

Sprinkle the soft brown sugar over the butter, bottom and sides

Arrange the pineapple rings around the base, having one in the middle and then the rest around it. Make sure that the outside ones go slightly up the sides too

Cut the glace cherries in half and place them inside the centre of each pineapple ring, cut side facing you

Put the caster sugar, self-raising flour, butter, baking powder, eggs (broken in), vanilla extract and golden syrup into a bowl and whisk well until light and fluffy

Pour the cake mix over the pineapple rings and spread evenly

KEY TIMER bake in the oven for 30-35 minutes (putting a skewer into the middle and should come out clean and no mix attached to it)

Carefully remove the cake and allow to cool a little

KEY very carefully put the plate on the top of the cake tin/bowl, bottom side up. Using a cloth in case it is hot, carefully flip the cake tin/bowl upside down so it now sits on the plate the right way up

Some may stick a bit, but that is ok, just rebuild any pieces that have stuck, back on

Serve warm or cold!

# Fruit Crumble

*Not just for winter!*

**Difficult rating:** ★★☆☆☆
**Serves:** 6
**Cooking time:** 20-25 mins
**Preparation time:** 30 mins
**Give Yourself Time:** 60 mins

**You Will Need**

*Large mixing bowl*
*Wooden spoon*
*Oven proof dish round or square and deep*
*Large saucepan*
*Metal spoon*
*Weighing scales*
*Knife*
*Chopping board*
*Zester*
*Teaspoon*
*Tablespoon*

## Ingredients

- 1kg ripe soft fruits of your choice (plums, apples, whatever) chopped into chunks (you can use any frozen mix you like here too
- 50g golden caster sugar
- 1 orange zested and juice
- 1 tspn ground cinnamon

For the topping

- 200g gluten free oats
- 2 tbspns butter at room temp
- Pinch mixed spice
- 2 tbspns maple syrup
- ½ tspn salt

**Hints & Tips**

You can make up the fruit mix a day ahead. Once cooled, just put it into an airtight container in the fridge until you need it

**Ways To Change**

Use different fruits

Put some nuts and seeds into your crumble mix for added crunch

## Method

KEY preheat oven to 200C

Put all of the crumble topping ingredients into a large bowl and combine with your hands

Rub the butter in between your fingers to create crumb type structure

In a sauce pan add the chopped fruit, sugar, orange zest and juice, cinnamon and heat until the sugar has dissolved

KEY TIMER Reduce the heat and simmer for 5 mins

Put the fruit mix into the oven dish and spread evenly

Scatter the crumble topping over

KEY TIMER bake for 20 mins until brown on top and bubbling at the sides

Serve with ice cream, custard or cream

# My Girl's Whoopee Pies

*Just because....!*

**Difficult rating:** ★★★☆☆
**Makes:** 12
**Cooking time:** 10 mins
**Preparation time:** 15 mins
**Give Yourself Time:** 35 mins

## You Will Need

*Weighing scales*
*Measuring jug*
*Large mixing bowl*
*Whisk*
*Fork*
*Teaspoon*
*2 baking trays*
*Greaseproof paper*
*Scissors*
*Metal tablespoon*
*Bowl to whisk egg in*

## Ingredients

- 125g gluten free plain flour
- ½ teaspoon xanthum gum
- 25g cocoa powder
- ½ tspn gluten free bicarb of soda
- ¼ tspn salt
- 110g light brown sugar
- 30g butter melted
- 25g coconut oil
- 1 free range egg
- 1 tspn vanilla extract
- 150ml milk
- ¼ tspn gluten free baking powder

## Hints & Tips

You are making 12 whoopee pies but that needs 24 sides – don't forget

Don't crowd them on the baking trays as they will spread a bit and join up if you aren't careful

## Ways To Change

Some chopped strawberries mixed in with the filling is lovely

You can even make one massive whoopee pie! Just put half the mixture on one tray, the other on the other and make sure reasonably similar in size and thickness. Fill it and serve as a whoopee pie cake!

## Method

KEY preheat the oven to 180C

Line the 2 baking trays with greaseproof paper across the bottoms of both

In the mixing bowl, add the flour, xanthum gum, cocoa powder, baking powder, bicarb of soda, salt and sugar and combine well

Add the melted butter and coconut oil and mix well using a fork to break up any lumps

Whisk the egg and add to the main bowl, together with the vanilla extract and milk

Whisk to combine to a smooth consistency

KEY using a metal tablespoon, add the batter to each baking tray in about 1 ½ inch wide circles. Put 12 onto each tray (2 together for each completed pie)

KEY make sure each circle is at least 1 inch apart from any others as they will spread a bit

KEY TIMER bake in the oven for 8-10 minutes then get them out to cool in the trays.

Move onto wire racks if you have them to cool further when able to touch

You now have 24 halves, just to stick them together!

Try some whisked double cream and a ¼ tspn vanilla extract in – get to reasonably stiff so doesn't drip out

Use just good old squirty cream to fill

Even whisked up custard is great

KEY Put your desired filling **onto half of the pies only**

Then place the other halves on top – finding the ones that match best in shape and size

Eat!

# Mum's Bread & Butter Pudding

*Her all time fave!*

**Difficult rating:** ★★★☆☆
**Serves:** 6-8
**Cooking time:** 40 mins
**Preparation time:** 20 mins
**Give Yourself Time:** 75 mins

**You Will Need**

*8 inch square shallow ovenproof dish you can serve it in*
*Knife*
*Chopping board*
*Zester*
*Whisk*
*2 mixing bowls*
*Weighing scales*
*Measuring jug*
*Cup*

## Ingredients

- 10-12 slices of gluten free white bread (older the better without being mouldy!)
- 600ml double cream
- 2 large free range eggs
- 25g butter at room temperature
- 25g caster sugar or brown sugar
- Zest of 1 orange
- Zest of 1 lemon
- 1 cup dried raisins
- Extra butter for greasing

## Method

KEY preheat the oven to 180C

Using the butter for greasing, spread it around the base and sides of the dish so lightly covered

Butter the bread on one side then cut into ¼ s in triangles

Arrange the triangles evenly in rows in the baking dish, pointy side up

Scatter the dried raisins all over the bread

In a bowl, put the cream, broken eggs, sugar, orange and lemon zests in and whisk to combine well

Pour this mixture over the bread triangles so equally covered

If you have time, put this in the fridge for half an hour before but it is not essential

KEY TIMER bake in the oven for 40 mins until golden brown and a little wobble in the middle

Serve hot, warm or even cold!

### Hints & Tips

Make this a little ahead and put in the fridge for at least 30 mins to really get the mix into the bread, but don't leave too long or have a soggy mess!

### Ways To Change

Use different types of gluten free bread-

Chilli fruit loaf is amazing

Brown or seeded

Brioche, if you can find it!

Use different dried fruits

Cranberries

Mixed

Candied fruit

# Sunken Chocolate Cake

*A real crowd pleaser!*

**Difficult rating:** ★★★★☆
**Serves:** 8 (or 6 greedies)
**Cooking time:** 70 mins
**Preparation time:** 25 mins
**Give Yourself Time:** 110 mins

### You Will Need

*2 large mixing bowls*
*2 small mixing bowls*
*8 × 4 inch round cake tin with loose bottom*
*Whisk (electric if have)*
*Saucepan*
*Greaseproof paper*
*Scissors*
*Spatula*
*Weighing scales*
*Measuring jug*

### Ingredients

- 6 small or 5 medium free range eggs
- 250g butter at room temp
- 250g dark chocolate – min 70% cocoa broken into pieces
- 250g caster sugar (golden if can but normal is fine)

### Method

KEY preheat the oven to 180C

Line the cake tin with greaseproof paper, bottom and sides right up

Put a saucepan half full of water onto a low simmer – not boiling

KEY put a small mixing bowl over the pan, making sure the **bottom does not touch the water in the pan**

Add the chocolate pieces and butter to the bowl and slowly let it melt

When melted, remove and set aside to cool a bit but not go cold and stiff

In separate bowls, separate the eggs, so whites into one bowl and yolks into another

KEY the best way I find is to break the egg into your fingers (loosely open) and letting the white fall through, then drop the yolk into the other

Add half (125g) of the sugar to the egg yolks and whisk until creamy and grown in volume

KEY In a separate bowl and **using a clean whisk (very important)** whisk the egg whites until you get stiff peaks

### Hints & Tips

Make sure you have either 2 whisks or clean the one you have used thoroughly and dry completely before whisking the egg white.

Make sure you keep the egg whites and the yolks well separate and know which is for which when following the recipe

### Ways To Change

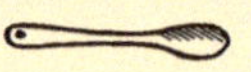

Put what you like really into the sunken hole – it is quite rich so fruit is great

Add in the other half of the sugar (125g) a little bit at a time, every 15-20 seconds, and keep whisking until it is all in and no grains

KEY Using a spatula, carefully stir in the chocolate mix to the **egg yolk** mix

KEY now carefully fold in the egg white mix to the chocolate mix, taking care to ensure all whites are gone but don't beat it and lose the air – gentle!

KEY TIMER pour the entire mix into the cake tin and bake for 65-70 mins

Remove the tin from the oven and let the cake cool whilst still in the tin

KEY it will sink........it's a sunken cake!

Carefully remove from the tin using the loose bottom and slide onto a serving plate.

You can serve as it is or pile on some whipped double cream or squirty cream or even custard

I like to fill ours with chopped strawberries and raspberries and then dollop some cream on top!

# Fruit Muffins

*Add your favourite fruits!*

**Difficult rating:** ★★★☆☆
**Makes:** 12
**Cooking time:** 20 mins
**Preparation time:** 15 mins
**Give Yourself Time:** 40 mins

**You Will Need**

*12 hole muffin tin or 2 × 6*
*12 paper muffin cases*
*Metal spoon*
*Whisk*
*2 × mixing bowls*
*Weighing scales*
*Measuring jug*
*Teaspoon*

## Ingredients

- 440g gluten free plain flour
- 160g caster sugar
- 60g soft butter (just melted)
- 2 free range eggs
- 165 ml plain natural yoghurt
- 1 tspn xanthum gum
- 1 tspn gluten free bicarb of soda
- ½ tspn ground nutmeg
- 1 tspn vanilla extract
- 300g of your favourite fruit chopped into small pieces
  strawberries, raisins, cherries, blueberries. raspberries, tropical, up to you!
  You can use frozen, just make sure fully defrosted first

**Hints & Tips**

If you wet your finger before dropping the mixture into the muffin papers, it is easier to get it off the spoon

Don't fill the cases right up as they will rise

**Ways To Change**

Use the fruits of your choice but try mix it up a bit

## Method

KEY preheat the oven to 190C

In one bowl, mix the flour, xanthum gum, sugar, bicarb of soda and nutmeg

In the 2nd bowl give the eggs a quick whisk and add the yoghurt, melted butter and vanilla extract and whisk together

Combine the 2 bowls together, one into the other, whichever way around you want

Mix in your chosen fruit and combine well

KEY Carefully spoon the mixture into the muffin cases, **filling each about 2/3rds up**

KEY TIMER put the tray in the oven for 18-20 minutes

Carefully remove and leave to cool on a wire rack if you have one

Enjoy warm or cold

# Fruit Salad

*A classic but always fantastic!*

**Difficult rating:** ★★☆☆☆
**Serves:** 4-6
**Cooking time:** 0 mins
**Preparation time:** 15 mins
**Give Yourself Time:** 25 mins

**You Will Need**

*Knife*
*Chopping board*
*Metal spoon*
*Large serving bowl*
*Weighing scales*
*Zester*
*Tablespoon*

### Ingredients

- 2 oranges peeled and cut into segments
- 100g blueberries
- 100g strawberries topped and cut in half
- ½ cantaloupe or gala melon – skin off and cut into bitesize chinks
- 500g frozen mixed tropical fruit (thawed from night before)
- 1 lemon or lime zested and juiced
- Splash of warm water (2 tbspns) and pinch of sugar – sugar dissolved in water

**Hints & Tips**

Make sure you remember to thaw the frozen fruit out overnight in the fridge

**Ways To Change**

Use different fruits

Add some fresh mint to the final dish for a fragrant kick

A pinch of chilli flakes goes a long way, I promise!

### Method

Put all of the fruit into the serving bowl and mix carefully so as not to break it up too much

Add the zest and juice of the lemon or lime

Stir in the water/sugar mix gently and serve with ice cream or cream

Party
Time

# Baked Tortilla Chips & Salsa

*Could not be easier!*

**Difficult rating:** ★☆☆☆☆
**Serves:** 4-6
**Cooking time:** 25 mins
**Preparation time:** 10 mins
**Give Yourself Time:** 40 mins

### You Will Need

*1 large casserole dish*
*Knife*
*Tablespoon*
*Chopping board*

### Ingredients

- 1 family sized bag gluten free tortilla chips
- 1 bag grated cheese
- 1 or 2 jars tomato salsa

### Method

KEY pre heat oven to 200C

Put half the bag of tortilla chips into the casserole dish and try to keep to same level

Add ½ of the tomato salsa across the top, allowing it to run down within the chips

Add half of the cheese across the top

Add the remainder of the tortilla chips

Add the remaining salsa and cheese topping

KEY TIMER bake in the oven for 20-25 mins until the cheese is brown and the salsa us bubbling

Serve with sour cream or crème freche and guacamole *(see recipe on page 130)*

### Hints & Tips

It is best served hot to warm

If it starts to get cold and there is some left (unlikely) just pop it back in the oven for 5 mins and you are ready to go again

You can also just keep topping it up, layers on layers, then back in the oven, to keep going through the party

### Ways To Change

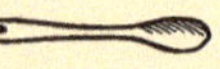

Try different types of gluten free flavoured tortilla chips

Try different types of grated cheese – chilli cheese, mozzarella, mix it up

Use different salsa heats for spice

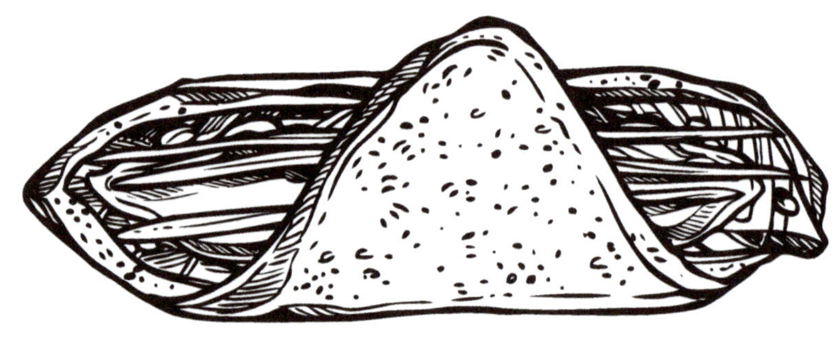

# My Girl's Family Tortizzas!

*The thinnest of thin crust!*

**Difficult rating:** ★☆☆☆☆
**Serves:** as many as make!
**Cooking time:** 15 mins
**Preparation time:** 10 mins
**Give Yourself Time:** 30 mins

### You Will Need

*2 baking trays*
*Knife*
*Chopping Board*
*Teaspoon*

### Ingredients

- 4 gluten free tortilla wraps
- Bag grated cheese
- Tomato pizza sauce *(see recipe on page 92)*

### Method

KEY preheat oven to 200C

Put the wraps onto the baking trays, 2 on each separated

Spread the tomato sauce onto the wraps, making sure to leave a 1cm edge free around each one for crispy crusts

Sprinkle on the grated cheese

KEY TIMER put the trays into the oven for 15 mins until the cheese is brown

Remove, slice and serve!

### Hints & Tips

Don't overload the tortizza with toppings or cheese as it will just stay soggy in the middle and crispy at the edges

### Ways To Change

This is a basic cheese and tomato tortizza so add some of your favourite toppings - bacon, mushroom, ham, chorizo, you name it

# My Girl's Party Tortizzas

*Party time all the time*

**Difficult rating:** ★☆☆☆☆
**Serves:** as many as you want
**Cooking time:** 5-10 mins
**Preparation time:** 10 mins
**Give Yourself Time:** 25 mins

## You Will Need

*2 baking trays*
*Knife*
*Chopping Board*
*Teaspoon*
*Small glass or cup or pastry circle cutter*

## Ingredients

4 gluten free tortilla wraps

Bag grated cheese

Tomato pizza sauce *(see recipe on page 92)*

Small glass or cup or pastry cutter

## Method

**KEY** preheat oven to 200C

On the chopping board, put your first wrap on

Taking either the cutter or the cup/glass, press down the open edge to cut into the wrap and create a small circle of wrap

Cut out as many as you can and then repeat with the other wraps

Put the circles of wraps onto the baking trays

Spread the tomato sauce onto the wrap circles, making sure to leave a small edge free around each one for crispy crusts

Sprinkle on the grated cheese

**KEY TIMER** put the trays into the oven for 5-10 mins until the cheese is brown

Remove and serve!

## Hints & Tips

These are small so will cook quicker than the bigger ones

Don't overload these tiny fellas as they will just go soggy, less is more!

## Ways To Change

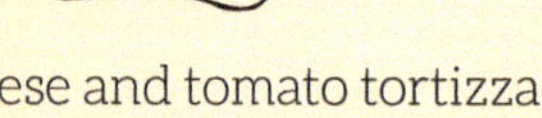

This is a basic cheese and tomato tortizza so add some of your favourite toppings - bacon, mushroom, ham, chorizo, you name it

# Ham & Egg Bakes

*So simple but delicious – party or not!*

**Difficult rating:** ★☆☆☆☆
**Makes:** 12
**Cooking time:** 15 mins
**Preparation time:** 10 mins
**Give Yourself Time:** 35 mins

**You Will Need**

*1 × 12 hole or 2 × 6 hole deep muffin trays*

## Ingredients

- 12 free range eggs
- 12 slices good quality ham (not processed thin slices)
- Splash single cream
- Salt & pepper
- Rapeseed oil for lining holes

## Method

KEY preheat oven to 180C

Dribble a little oil into each of the muffin tray holes, wiping it around the entire insides of each with your finger

KEY Take a slice of the ham and place it over the first hole and carefully push it down so it fills the base and sides and **must flop over the top sides**

This is the ham 'cup' to hold the egg so make sure it is holeless!

Carefully crack an egg into the ham 'cup

Add a splash of cream

Repeat for the remaining 11 holes

Sprinkle salt and pepper on top of each egg

KEY TIMER bake in the oven for 10-15 minutes until the eggs are just set (little wobbles)

Remove carefully from the oven

Carefully lift each ham/egg cup out using the ham that is spilling over each one

The ham should stand up on its own now with the baked egg inside

Serve hot or warm

### Hints & Tips

Try and make sure the ham lining of the holes is full and there are no holes for the egg to seep out of whilst cooking

Make sure the ham is flopped well over the sides as creates the handle for the cups to get them out

### Ways To Change

Add a dash of tobasco on top of the cream for a kick

Or add some chilli flakes on top

Or add some smoked paprika on top

# Fruit Brulees

*So easy & wonderful*

**Difficult rating:** ★☆☆☆☆
**Serves:** 4
**Cooking time:** 10 mins
**Preparation time:** 10 mins
**Give Yourself Time:** 25 mins

**You Will Need**

*Knife*
*Chopping board*
*Shallow oven dish*
*Teaspoon*

## Ingredients

- 4 ripe peaches
- 8 tspns caster sugar
- 8 tspns soft gluten free plain cream cheese

## Method

KEY preheat grill to hot

Carefully cut the peaches into halves and place into the oven dish open side up

Remove the stones

In each peach half put a tspn of the cream cheese in the hole where the stone was

Sprinkle a teaspoon of caster sugar on top of the cream cheese for each

Put under the hot grill until the sugar is brown

Serve nice and warm with some ice cream

### Hints & Tips

Be very careful, hot sugar melted is lethal so keep your hands away

### Ways To Change

Use any ripe fruit that has a stone hole to use - nectarines, plums etc

Sprinkle little chilli flakes on top of each with the sugar

# Handies

# Cheese Sauce

## Quick Cheats one

*When in a real rush!*

**Difficult rating:** ★☆☆☆☆
**Serves:** 4-6
**Cooking time:** 5 mins
**Preparation time:** 5 mins
**Give Yourself Time:** 15 mins

### You Will Need

*Sauce pan*
*Wooden spoon*
*Teaspoon*
*Cup*

### Ingredients

- 1 packet of gluten free cream cheese
- 1 cup of water (or retained water used for cooking pasta)

### Method

If cooking pasta at the same time, drain the pasta when done but keep back a cup full of the cooking water

If making from scratch just add a cup full of water to a pan

Put the heat to medium to get the water nice and hot

Add the tub of cream cheese and stir well to combine and heat up

One very easy cheese sauce now made

### Hints & Tips

If the sauce is too thick just add a bit more water

If you need to make a lot, just double everything

It can be made ahead and left with the lid on for a few hours until you need it

### Ways To Change

Use different flavours of cream cheese, ie garlic and herb, chili etc to get different flavoured sauces

# Full Cheese Sauce

*Once mastered you will use this a lot!*

**Difficult rating:** ★★★☆☆
**Serves:** 6
**Cooking time:** 10 mins
**Preparation time:** 10 mins
**Give Yourself Time:** 30 mins

**You Will Need**

*Large saucepan*
*Whisk*
*Measuring jug*
*Weighing scales*
*Wooden spoon*
*Teaspoon*
*Tablespoon*

## Ingredients

- 4 tbspns gluten free plain flour
- 50g butter
- 500ml milk – use full fat or semi if can
- 100g grated cheese
- 1 tspn English mustard

## Method

Put the saucepan onto a medium heat and add the butter to melt

KEY When fully melted and starting to heat up, add the flour and stir continuously until you get a gooey yellow paste

Add a splash of the milk and keep stirring to combine and work out any lumps

Add a little more of the milk and continue to stir and combine and get out any lumps

Slowly keep adding the milk and stirring, milk and stirring until all is in and there are no lumps

If you do get any lumps, just use the whisk to beat them out and then back to the wooden spoon

KEY Keep stirring but do not let the milk boil it will slowly start to thicken

KEY When it looks like it may boil and the sauce is thickened a bit, take it off the heat

Stir in the grated cheese and mustard to a smooth consistency

Use as you need

### Hints & Tips

Never let the milk boil – simmer is as far as it can go

You have to keep stirring so this one really is a work out and need to be ready for it!

Once cold you can freeze this and use then as you need it

### Ways To Change

Increase the amount of mustard for more background heat

Put a pinch of nutmeg in

Try different grated cheeses for different flavours of sauce

# Coleslaws - Classic

*Works every time and so versatile*

**Difficult rating:** ★★☆☆☆
**Serves:** 4-6 as side
**Cooking time:** 0 mins
**Preparation time:** 15 mins
**Give Yourself Time:** 20 mins

**You Will Need**

*Knife*
*Chopping board*
*Large mixing bowl*
*Tablespoon*
*Teaspoon*
*Vegetable peeler*
*Grater*
*Metal spoon*

## Ingredients

- ½ white cabbage
- 1 carrot peeled
- 3 spring onions
- 1 tspn English mustard
- 4 tbspns mayonnaise
- 1-2 tspns cider or white wine vinegar
- Salt & pepper

**Hints & Tips**

Get everything as fine as you can as makes eating a whole lot easier - take your time

Serve it when you have made it really as fresh is best - you can keep in the fridge for a bit before though

**Ways To Change**

See following recipes

## Method

If you have a whole cabbage, cut it into half, then the half you will use, half it again. Cut out the central stalk part as it is tough and not nice to eat

Slice the cabbage as finely as you can into strips and add to the bowl

Grate the carrot on the largest setting and add to the bowl

Chop the spring onion / scallions into small rounds and add to the bowl

Add the mayonnaise, mustard, vinegar and salt and pepper to the bowl and mix well with your hands or a metal spoon

Serve how you wish

# Coleslaws – Red Cabbage

*Works every time and so versatile*

**Difficult rating:** ★★☆☆☆
**Serves:** 4-6 as side
**Cooking time:** 0 mins
**Preparation time:** 15 mins
**Give Yourself Time:** 20 mins

**You Will Need**

| | | |
|---|---|---|
| *Knife* | *Tablespoon* | *Grater* |
| *Chopping board* | *Teaspoon* | *Zester* |
| *Large mixing bowl* | *Vegetable peeler* | *Metal spoon* |

## Ingredients

- ¼ white cabbage
- 1 carrot peeled
- ¼ red cabbage
- 1 lime zested and juiced
- 3 spring onions
- 1 tspn Dijon mustard
- 4 tbspns mayonnaise
- 1-2 tspns cider or white wine vinegar
- Salt & pepper
- Pinch of sugar

## Hints & Tips

Get everything as fine as you can as makes eating a whole lot easier - take your time

Serve it when you have made it really as fresh is best - you can keep in the fridge for a bit before though

KEY here is that the white cabbage from the classic recipe has dropped from a ½ to a ¼ , and the mustard is Dijon not English

## Method

If you have whole cabbages, cut it into half, then half again. On the ¼ of each you will use cut out the central stalk part as it is tough and not nice to eat

Slice both white and red cabbage as finely as you can into strips and add to the bowl

Grate the carrot on the largest setting and add to the bowl

Chop the spring onion / scallions into small rounds and add to the bowl

Add the mayonnaise, vinegar, mustard, lime zest and juice, sugar and salt and pepper to the bowl and mix well with your hands or a metal spoon

Serve how you wish

# Coleslaws – Curry

*Works every time and so versatile*

**Difficult rating:** ★★☆☆☆
**Serves:** 4-6 as side
**Cooking time:** 0 mins
**Preparation time:** 15 mins
**Give Yourself Time:** 20 mins

## You Will Need

*Knife*
*Chopping board*
*Large mixing bowl*
*Tablespoon*
*Teaspoon*
*Vegetable peeler*
*Grater*
*Zester*
*Cup*
*Metal spoon*

## Ingredients

- ¼ white cabbage
- 1 carrot peeled
- ¼ red cabbage
- 1 lime zested and juiced
- 3 spring onions
- 1 tspn Dijon mustard
- 4 tbspns mayonnaise
- 1-2 tspns cider or white wine vinegar
- Salt & pepper
- Pinch of sugar
- 1 tspn curry powder

### Hints & Tips

Get everything as fine as you can as makes eating a whole lot easier – take your time

Serve it when you have made it really as fresh is best – you can keep in the fridge for a bit before though

## Method

If you have whole cabbages, cut it into half, then half again. On the ¼ of each you will use cut out the central stalk part as it is tough and not nice to eat

Slice both white and red cabbage as finely as you can into strips and add to the bowl

Grate the carrot on the largest setting and add to the bowl

Chop the spring onion / scallions into small rounds and add to the bowl

Add the curry powder, mayonnaise, vinegar, mustard, lime zest and juice, sugar and salt and pepper to the bowl and mix well with your hands or a metal spoon

Serve how you wish

# Coleslaws – Fruit & Nut

*Works every time and so versatile*

**Difficult rating:** ★★☆☆☆
**Serves:** 4-6 as side
**Cooking time:** 0 mins
**Preparation time:** 15 mins
**Give Yourself Time:** 20 mins

**You Will Need**

*Knife*
*Chopping board*
*Large mixing bowl*
*Tablespoon*
*Teaspoon*
*Vegetable peeler*
*Grater*
*Zester*
*Cup*
*Metal spoon*

## Ingredients

- ¼ white cabbage
- 1 carrot peeled
- ¼ red cabbage
- 1 lime zested and juiced
- 3 spring onions
- 1 tspn Dijon mustard
- 4 tbspns mayonnaise
- 1-2 tspns cider or white wine vinegar
- Salt & pepper
- Pinch of sugar
- Handful of dried raisins
- Handful of dried apricots chopped
- ¼ cup mixed seeds – linseed, chia, pumpkin etc
- ¼ cup chopped mixed nuts – peanut, pistachio, almond etc

**Hints & Tips**

Get everything as fine as you can as makes eating a whole lot easier – take your time

Serve it when you have made it really as fresh is best – you can keep in the fridge for a bit before though

If this is getting a bit dry, add some more mayo and / or mustard

## Method

If you have whole cabbages, cut it into half, then half again. On the ¼ of each you will use cut out the central stalk part as it is tough and not nice to eat

Slice both white and red cabbage as finely as you can into strips and add to the bowl

Grate the carrot on the largest setting and add to the bowl

Chop the spring onion / scallions into small rounds and add to the bowl

Add the raisins, apricots, mixed seeds and nuts to the bowl and combine well

Add the mayonnaise, vinegar, mustard, lime zest and juice, sugar and salt and pepper to the bowl and mix well with your hands or a metal spoon

Serve how you wish

# Coleslaws – Spicy

*Works every time and so versatile*

**Difficult rating:** ★★☆☆☆
**Serves:** 4-6 as side
**Cooking time:** 0 mins
**Preparation time:** 15 mins
**Give Yourself Time:** 20 mins

**You Will Need**

*Knife*
*Chopping board*
*Large mixing bowl*
*Tablespoon*
*Teaspoon*
*Vegetable peeler*
*Grater*
*Zester*
*Cup*
*Metal spoon*

## Ingredients

- ¼ white cabbage
- 1 carrot peeled
- ¼ red cabbage
- 1 lime zested and juiced
- 3 spring onions
- 1 tspn Dijon mustard
- 4 tbspns mayonnaise
- 1-2 tspns cider or white wine vinegar
- Salt & pepper
- Pinch of sugar
- 2 red chillis, chopped (watch the heat levels)

## Method

If you have whole cabbages, cut it into half, then half again. On the ¼ of each you will use cut out the central stalk part as it is tough and not nice to eat

Slice both white and red cabbage as finely as you can into strips and add to the bowl

Grate the carrot on the largest setting and add to the bowl

Chop the spring onion / scallions into small rounds and add to the bowl

Add the chillis, mayonnaise, vinegar, mustard, lime zest and juice, sugar and salt and pepper to the bowl and mix well with your hands or a metal spoon

Serve how you wish

### Hints & Tips

Get everything as fine as you can as makes eating a whole lot easier - take your time

Serve it when you have made it really as fresh is best - you can keep in the fridge for a bit before though

**KEY** here is that the white cabbage from the classic recipe has dropped from a ½ to a ¼ , and the mustard is Dijon not English

You can add the chillis to any of these, here it is the red cabbage recipe I have used

Be careful with chillis - if you are not sure, taste a very small part for the heat. Generally, the smaller the more fiery. Removing seeds and the sinu can help reduce heat

# Garlic Bread

*I used to love making bread, but since being diagnosed coeliac that has changed!*
*It is more of a chemistry lesson than baking!*
*So, yes, I buy it!*
*You can still upgrade it though!*

**Difficult rating:** ★☆☆☆☆
**Serves:** 4-8
**Cooking time:** 10-15 mins
**Preparation time:** 10 mins
**Give Yourself Time:** 30 mins

**You Will Need**

*Tablespoon*
*Knife*
*Chopping Board*
*Teaspoon*
*Baking tray*
*Small bowl*

### Ingredients

- 1 or 2 gluten free baguettes or rolls
- 4 tbspns room temp butter (8 if doing two baguettes)
- 2 tspns chopped garlic (4 if doing two baguettes)
- (optional) 1 tspn chopped coriander (frozen good too)

### Method

KEY preheat the oven to 200C

KEY With a knife, carefully make cuts into the baguettes or rolls that go about ¾ s way down – **not all the way through**

Make the cuts along the bread in approx. 2 cm intervals

Add the softened butter to a bowl

Add the garlic and coriander (if using) and mix well with a teaspoon

Carefully now spoon the butter mix into the slashes in the bread making sure you get right in but not breaking the bread apart. A good heaped teaspoonful into each

Once all is in, give the bread a little squish to push the ends together a bit so the bread gaps push together but not so the filling comes out

If you have any filling left over, spread it across the top of the bread

KEY TIMER put in the oven for 10-15 mins (check the instructions of the bread – if part baked it may take longer)

Remove, slice and enjoy!

### Hints & Tips

If you run out of butter and garlic mix, just make some more!

You can make the garlic butter way ahead, it will keep in the fridge in a sealed container for a few days. Just remember it will smell of garlic so ensure it is tightly shut!

### Ways To Change

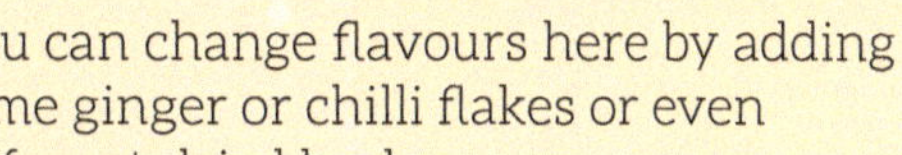

You can change flavours here by adding some ginger or chilli flakes or even different dried herbs

# Easy Guacamole

*Better than anything you will buy!*

**Difficult rating:** ★★☆☆☆
**Serves:** 6 as a side
**Cooking time:** 0 mins
**Preparation time:** 10 mins
**Give Yourself Time:** 15 mins

**You Will Need**

*Knife*
*Chopping board*
*Mixing bowl*
*Teaspoon*
*Zester*
*Fork*

## Ingredients

- 1 ripe avocado
- ½ red or white onion chopped finely (frozen ok as long as thaw well)
- 1 big ripe tomato chopped finely
- 1 lime zested and juiced
- 1 tspn chopped garlic
- Salt and pepper

## Method

Cut the avocado in half lengthways around the stone

Twist the 2 halves so they come apart

Remove the flesh from each side using a teaspoon to run around the inside of the skin to release each side.

Scoop the stone out

Put the flesh into a bowl and squash with the back of a fork to break up

Add all of the remaining ingredients and combine well with a fork

Serve with whatever dish you are accompanying

### Hints & Tips

Getting the stone out of one side of the avocado you can either use a spoon to scoop it out or bang it with a sharp knife (carefully) and it will lift out

It will keep in a sealed airtight container for a couple of days as the lime juice will keep the avocado from browning

### Ways To Change

Add some chillis

Some fresh coriander torn into it is lovely

# Herb Green Pesto

*So versatile and, once you've made this yourself, you won't buy a pot again!*

**Difficult rating:** ★☆☆☆☆
**Serves:** quite a lot!
**Cooking time:** 0 mins
**Preparation time:** 10 mins
**Give Yourself Time:** 15 mins

## You Will Need

*Blender*
*Weighing scales*
*Tablespoon*
*Frying pan*

## Ingredients

- 50g pine nuts
- 50g parmesan cheese grated
- 1 tspn chopped garlic
- 150ml extra virgin olive oil
- 2 handfuls of fresh basil
- Salt & pepper

## Method

KEY Put the pine nuts into the frying pan and warm gently over a low heat but with **NO oil**, use a dry pan.

KEY keep an eye on them as they will brown quickly and take them off the heat and out of the pan to set aside as soon as they are toasted

Put the pine nuts, basil, parmesan, garlic and olive oil into the blender and whizz until either smooth or a little chunky (if you prefer it that way)

Taste and season with salt and pepper to your taste

Use it how you want to!

## Hints & Tips

This keeps in a sealed container for a good week so make it and use it!

Use a dry pan for toasting the pine nuts

## Ways To Change

You can use this as a great topping to a stew – just add right at the end to the top and let people mix in their own

As a topping to some plain gluten free pasta it is delightful!

# Infused Oils

*Fantastic & so easy to do!*

**Difficult rating:** ★☆☆☆☆

Extra virgin olive oil is a real need for a salad, just drizzled over leaves it can make a massive difference to the taste. It also adds flavour to hot food like stir fries etc. **However**, you can really enhance the natural flavour of olive oil, or indeed rapeseed oil if you prefer that, with some very simple methods, as follows.

If you are lucky enough to have bottles available (using old olive oil bottles is the best so don't throw them away when you are empty), or any oil container then use them. You can though do this in a mug or even into a re-usable zip locked freezer bag!

**You Will Need**

*Some reasonably good quality extra virgin olive oil*

*One or more of the following infusers*

## Lemon Oil

**Method**

Take 1-2 lemons and carefully peel off the skin

Cut into ¼ s

Put the skin and ¼ 'd flesh into your bottle, mug or bag

Pour over the oil and leave to infuse

The longer you can leave this the more flavour you will get into the oil

It will keep for a very long time!

## Thyme Oil

**Method**

**KEY** Take 4-5 sprigs of fresh thyme – not dried

Add to the bottle, mug or bag

Pour over the oil and leave to infuse

The longer you can leave this the more flavour you will get into the oil

It will keep for a very long time!

## Chilli Oil

**Method**

Take 3 or 4 hot red chillis and cut in ½'s

Pour over the oil and leave to infuse

KEY Please don't rub your eyes or anywhere else after cutting chillis – wash your hands

## Pepper Oil

**Method**

Take 1-2 fresh peppers of your choice and cut into ¼'s or a size you can get into your vessel

Add a tablespoon full of whole black peppercorns

Pour over the oil and leave to infuse

## Garlic Oil

**Method**

Take 5-6 garlic cloves – not chopped, but squash a little so they open up a bit and add to your vessel (cut if won't fit in)

Pour over the oil and leave to infuse

## Bay Leaf Oil

**Method**

Take 4-5 whole bay leaves and add to the vessel

Pour over the oil and leave to infuse

## Olive Olive Oil! (if you really love olives)

**Method**

Add a selection of olives – plain, garlic, chilli to your container

Pour over the oil and leave to infuse

## Mixed Herb Oil

**Method**

Add whole sprigs of your favourite hard herbs to your vessel – rosemary, thyme, bay

Pour over the oil and leave to infuse

**Hints & Tips**

You can use these oils in all kinds of dishes

- to salads they are great
- heated as a base for dishes like curries and stir fries, even omelettes

Experiment – it is really great fun!

# Roasted Vegetables

*A meal on their own or a great accompaniment to a meat or fish dish*

**Difficult rating:** ★★☆☆☆
**Serves:** 4
**Cooking time:** 20-25 mins
**Preparation time:** 10 mins
**Give Yourself Time:** 45 mins

### You Will Need

*Knife*
*Chopping board*
*Large mixing bowl*
*Baking tray (may need 2)*
*Tablespoon*
*Vegetable peeler*
*Tin foil*

### Ingredients

- 1 whole broccoli broken into small florets or packet of tender stem broccoli
- Salt and pepper
- 2 carrots, peeled and cut into large batons
- 2 parsnips peeled and cut into chunks
- 2 small maris piper potatoes peeled and diced
- 1 small swede peeled and diced
- 2 tbspns lemon juice
- 2 tbspns honey

### Method

KEY Preheat the oven to 200c fan

Place all of the mixed veg into a large bowl and season with salt and pepper

Add the honey and lemon juice and mix thoroughly so all covered

Lay the mixed veg onto a double foil lined baking tray

KEY TIMER Bake in the oven for 20-25 mins until cooked through – depends on size of the veg

### Hints & Tips

If the broccoli is starting to catch, lower the tray in the oven and cover with foil for the remaining time left

Cutting things to similar sizes helps ensure even cooking

### Ways To Change

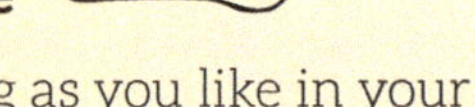

Use different veg as you like in your family

Add thickly sliced onion for more flavour

This is nice with a sour cream dip

A little balsamic vinegar in the honey and lemon mix is lovely too

# Home-Made Chips or Wedges

*Simple and delicious for all of the family*

**Difficult rating:** ★☆☆☆☆
**Serves:** 4
**Cooking time:** 25-30 mins
**Preparation time:** 10 mins
**Give Yourself Time:** 45 mins

**You Will Need**

*Knife*
*Chopping board*
*Vegetable peeler*
*Baking tray*

## Ingredients

- 5-6 good sized maris piper potatoes – peeled
- Rapeseed oil
- Salt

## Method

KEY Pre-heat the oven to 200c

### Chips

Cut the potatoes into even shaped chip sizes – of your choice

Spread onto a baking tray

Drizzle with the oil and toss throughout to ensure evenly covered all over

Sprinkle salt over the top

Ensure even layer of chips on the tray

KEY TIMER add to the oven for 25 – 30 mins until nice and golden brown

### Wedges

Cut the potatoes in ½ lengthways

With the potatoes flat side down, carefully cut triangle wedge shapes out and repeat for all of the potatoes

Spread onto a baking tray and drizzle with the oil and toss throughout to ensure evenly covered all over

Set them out with the wider side down so they are standing upright

Sprinkle salt over the top

KEY TIMER add to the oven for 25 – 30 mins until nice and golden brown

**Hints & Tips**

Try to cut the chips or wedges into similar sizes and shapes so they all cook at the same time

Keep a single layer of potatoes on the baking tray. If you have too many, use a second baking sheet and don't just pile them all on, as the lower level won't cook as well

**Ways To Change**

Add some curry spices for an Indian twist

Use sweet potatoes for a different flavour – but reduce the cooking time by 5-10 mins

# Roast Potato 4 Ways

## Roast Potatoes – Traditional

*(no par boiling or shaking here!)*
*Everyone is a winner!*

**Difficult rating:** ★★☆☆☆
**Serves:** 4-6
**Cooking time:** 60 mins
**Preparation time:** 15 mins
**Give Yourself Time:** 80 mins

### You Will Need

*Knife*
*Chopping board*
*Vegetable peeler*
*Baking tray*

### Ingredients

- 6 maris piper potatoes, peeled
- Rapeseed oil
- Salt

### Hints & Tips

Try and keep the potatoes the same size when chopping so they cook evenly

### Ways To Change

Use your infused oil for some added flavour

### Method

KEY preheat the oven to 200C
Cut the potatoes into ½ s (large ones into 3)
Put onto the baking tray
Drizzle with rapeseed oil and toss with your hands to ensure all are covered
Sprinkle salt over the potatoes
KEY TIMER put into the oven for 60 mins and are golden brown and crispy on the bottom

# Roast Potatoes – Curried

*(no par boiling or shaking here!)*
*Everyone is a winner!*

**Difficult rating:** ★★☆☆☆
**Serves:** 4-6
**Cooking time:** 60 mins
**Preparation time:** 15 mins
**Give Yourself Time:** 80 mins

### You Will Need

*Knife*
*Chopping board*
*Vegetable peeler*
*Baking tray*
*Teaspoon*

### Ingredients

- 6 maris piper potatoes, peeled
- Rapeseed oil
- Salt
- 2 tspns curry powder

### Hints & Tips

Try and keep the potatoes the same size when chopping so they cook evenly

### Ways To Change

Use your infused oil for some added flavour

### Method

**KEY** preheat the oven to 200C

Cut the potatoes into ½ s (large ones into 3)

Put onto the baking tray

Sprinkle over the curry powder, drizzle with rapeseed oil and toss with your hands to ensure all are covered

Sprinkle salt over the potatoes

**KEY TIMER** put into the oven for 60 mins and are golden brown and crispy on the bottom

# Roast Potatoes – Garlic & Herb

*(no par boiling or shaking here!)*
*Everyone is a winner!*

**Difficult rating:** ★★☆☆☆
**Serves:** 4-6
**Cooking time:** 60 mins
**Preparation time:** 15 mins
**Give Yourself Time:** 80 mins

**You Will Need**

*Knife*
*Chopping board*
*Vegetable peeler*
*Baking tray*
*Teaspoon*

**Hints & Tips**

Try and keep the potatoes the same size when chopping so they cook evenly

**Ways To Change**

Use your infused oil for some added flavour

## Ingredients

- 6 maris piper potatoes, peeled
- Rapeseed oil
- Salt
- 1 tspn dried chopped rosemary
- 1 tspn chopped garlic

## Method

KEY preheat the oven to 200C
Cut the potatoes into ½ s (large ones into 3)
Put onto the baking tray
Drizzle with rapeseed oil and toss with your hands to ensure all are covered
Add the rosemary and garlic and ensure well mixed through
Sprinkle salt over the potatoes
KEY TIMER put into the oven for 60 mins and are golden brown and crispy on the bottom

# Roast Potatoes – Paprika & Butter

*(no par boiling or shaking here!)*
*Everyone is a winner!*

**Difficult rating:** ★★☆☆☆
**Serves:** 4-6
**Cooking time:** 60 mins
**Preparation time:** 15 mins
**Give Yourself Time:** 80 mins

**You Will Need**

*Knife*
*Chopping board*
*Vegetable peeler*
*Baking tray*
*Teaspoon*

### Ingredients

- 6 maris piper potatoes, peeled
- Rapeseed oil
- Salt
- 2 tspns paprika (smoked or normal)
- 12 small knobs butter

### Method

KEY preheat the oven to 200C

Cut the potatoes into ½ s (large ones into 3)

Put onto the baking tray

Sprinkle over the paprika and drizzle with rapeseed oil and toss with your hands to ensure all are covered

Sprinkle salt over the potatoes and top with a knob of butter for each potato

KEY TIMER put into the oven for 60 mins and are golden brown and crispy on the bottom

### Hints & Tips

Try and keep the potatoes the same size when chopping so they cook evenly

### Ways To Change

Use your infused oil for some added flavour

# Chip Dips – Tomato 'Sauce'

*Instead of just ketchup – try these!*

**Difficult rating:** ★★½☆☆
**Serves:** 4-6
**Cooking time:** 10 mins
**Preparation time:** 15 mins
**Give Yourself Time:** 30 mins

**You Will Need**

*Knife*
*Chopping board*
*Teaspoon*
*Large frying pan*
*Cup*

## Ingredients

- 12 cherry / plum tomatoes cut into ¼ s
- 1 tspn chopped garlic
- 1 tspn chopped ginger
- ½ white onion peeled and chopped finely (1/2 cup frozen great too)
- 1 tspn gluten free Worcester sauce
- 1 tspn sugar or sweetener
- Salt & pepper

### Hints & Tips

Let it get nice and sticky!

You can keep this, once cooled, in an airtight container in the fridge for a week or so)

### Ways To Change

Add some chilli flakes for an extra kick

## Method

Put all of the ingredients into the frying pan

Fry over a medium heat until it is all bubbling

KEY Turn down the heat and leave to simmer gently until it starts to thicken

Add a splash of water if it is getting a bit dry

Serve as a dip hot or warm or cold

# Chip Dips – Chilli, Pepper & Feta

*Instead of just ketchup – try these!*

**Difficult rating:** ★☆☆☆☆
**Serves:** 4-6
**Cooking time:** 0 mins
**Preparation time:** 10 mins
**Give Yourself Time:** 15 mins

### You Will Need

*Knife*
*Chopping board*
*Teaspoon*
*Teaspoon*
*Blender*
*Mixing bowl*
*Weighing scales*

### Ingredients

- 1 jar red peppers (approx. 120g when out of the jar)
- 240g (or twice the weight of the peppers) of Feta cheese
- 2 tbspns extra virgin olive oil
- 1 tspn dried chilli flakes

### Method

Add all of the ingredients to the blender and whizz to creamy texture

Serve!

### Hints & Tips

It will keep in an airtight container in the fridge for a week

### Ways To Change 

You can use your infused pepper oil or any of the oils here to add more flavour

# Chip Dips – Pesto & Cream Cheese

*Instead of just ketchup – try these!*

**Difficult rating:** ★☆☆☆☆
**Serves:** 6-8
**Cooking time:** 0 mins
**Preparation time:** 10 mins
**Give Yourself Time:** 15 mins

**You Will Need**

*Bowl*
*Tablespoon*
*Spatula*

**Ingredients**

- 4 tbspns green herb pesto *(see recipe on page 131)*
- 2 tubs plain cream cheese

**Method**

Put the cream cheese into the bowl and give it a squash with a tablespoon

Swirl through the pesto and either leave as a ripple or combine fully and go green!

Serve

**Hints & Tips**

Give the cheese a good squash before you add the pesto

You can keep this in an airtight container in the fridge for a week or so)

# Chip Dips – Curry Mayo

*Instead of just ketchup – try these!*

**Difficult rating:** ★☆☆☆☆
**Serves:** 4-6
**Cooking time:** 0 mins
**Preparation time:** 5 mins
**Give Yourself Time:** 10 mins

**You Will Need**

*Mixing bowl*
*Teaspoon*
*Measuring scales*

**Ingredients**

- 130g mayonnaise
- 2-3 tspns curry powder

**Method**

Put both ingredients into a bowl and mix well

Serve

**Hints & Tips**

None!

You can keep this, once cooled, in an airtight container in the fridge for a week or so)

**Ways To Change**

Change the heat of your curry powder to suit your needs

# Yorkshire Puddings

*If you can get these to the table before being pinched you've done well!*

**Difficult rating:** ★★☆☆☆
**Serves:** Up to 6
**Cooking time:** 30 mins
**Preparation time:** 10 mins
**Give Yourself Time:** 45 mins

**You Will Need**

*12 hole Yorkshire pudding tin*
*Measuring scales*
*Measuring jug*
*Whisk*
*Large pouring jug / large bowl*
*Teaspoon*

## Ingredients

- 140g gluten free plain flour
- 50g corn flour
- 3 large free range eggs
- 175ml milk (whole or semi)
- Rapeseed oil
- Salt

## Method

KEY Pre heat the oven to 200C

Sift the flour into a bowl (preferably a large pouring jug as easier later)

Add a teaspoon of salt and mix well

Crack the 3 eggs directly into the flour mix

Whisk well until combined and little or no flour showing

Add the milk little by little, whisking well each time to ensure no lumps

KEY TIMER When all of the milk is combined set aside to rest for 15 mins minimum. Re whisk it again quickly just before adding to the hot tins

Put a dribble of rapeseed oil into the wells of a 12 hole yorkie tin

KEY TIMER When ready to cook, put the tray into the oven for 5 mins for the oil to get hot

Very carefully remove the tin (oil is lethally hot) and pour in the batter mix to each well until level with the top of each well

KEY TIMER Put the tray back in the oven and cook for 25 mins

Serve!

### Hints & Tips

Really whisk the mixture early to get any lumps out

The oil in the tins has to be nice and hot before adding the mix, otherwise it will stick and likely won't rise as well

### Ways To Change

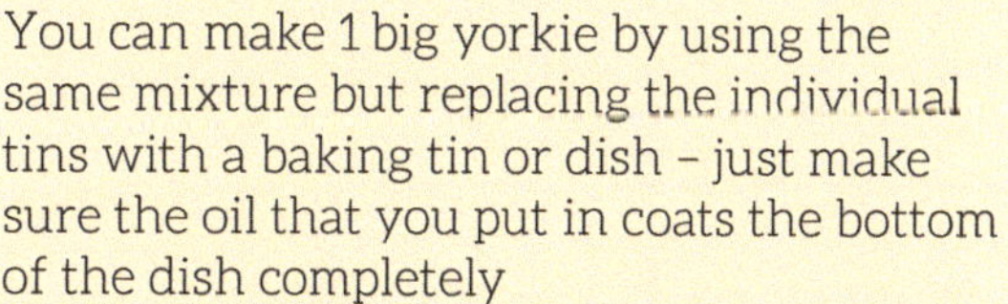

You can make 1 big yorkie by using the same mixture but replacing the individual tins with a baking tin or dish – just make sure the oil that you put in coats the bottom of the dish completely

You can make sweet versions of these *(see recipe on page 104)*

# Spiced Red Cabbage

*It's not just for Christmas!*

**Difficult rating:** ★★☆☆☆
**Serves:** Up to 8
**Cooking time:** 60 mins
**Preparation time:** 25 mins
**Give Yourself Time:** 95 mins

### You Will Need

*Knife*
*Chopping board*
*Weighing scales*
*Teaspoon*
*Zester*
*Large deep frying pan with lid*
*Measuring jug*
*Tablespoon*

### Ingredients

- 1 × large red cabbage
- 1 tbspn red wine vinegar
- 25g butter
- 150ml water
- 2 red onions, peeled and chopped as small as can get
- Pinch of mixed spice
- 1 × orange zested and juiced
- 1 × cinnamon stick
- 150ml port (optional – use water if for children)

### Hints & Tips

Prepare well in advance, even days before, cool and keep in the fridge or the freezer until needed

### Ways To Change

Add lemon zest for added zing

A touch of chilli flakes makes it lovely and warming!

### Method

Cut the red cabbage into thin slices (long and thin is best) – remove the core makes it less tough

KEY TIMER Gently fry the red onions in the butter in a large pan for 5-10 mins

KEY Add the orange zest, mixed spice and cinnamon stick and cook for a further minute

Add the shredded cabbage and stir through fully

Add the port (or water), red wine vinegar and orange zest

Add the water (or double amount of water if no port), stir and bring to the boil

KEY TIMER Reduce the heat to a slow simmer, cover and cook for 45 mins or so until cabbage nice and soft

# In Bag Marinades

*Great for the fridge – less mess*

**Difficult rating:** ★☆☆☆☆
**Cooking time:** 0 mins
**Preparation time:** 5 mins
**Give Yourself Time:** 10 mins

**You Will Need**

*Large zip lock freezer bags*
*Space in the fridge*
*The meat of your choice*
*One of the following*
*Tablespoon*
*Teaspoon*
*Zester*

The following recipes of marinades will work with most meats and fish to get extra flavour in before cooking

## Tandoori Yoghurt

### Ingredients

- 3 tbspns natural full fat yoghurt (plain)
- 2 tspns tandoori spice
- Pinch salt

### Method

Put all ingredients into the bag

Add the meat of your choice as you will be cooking it, ie strips, chunks, whole

Close the bag getting as much of the air out before you zip it up

Gently massage the mix together and around the meat so it is completely covered

KEY Leave for a minimum of an hour but preferably in the fridge overnight

When you are ready to cook, take the meat out of the bag and remove any excess marinade

Cook as you wish!

## Garlic & Herb

### Ingredients

- 2 teaspoons chopped garlic
- 1 tbspn mixed dried herbs (Italian or mixed)
- 2 tbspns rapeseed or olive oil

### Method

Put all ingredients into the bag

Add the meat of your choice as you will be cooking it, ie strips, chunks, whole

Close the bag getting as much of the air out before you zip it up

Gently massage the mix together and around the meat so it is completely covered

KEY Leave for a minimum of an hour but preferably in the fridge overnight

When you are ready to cook, take the meat out of the bag and remove any excess marinade

Cook as you wish!

### Hints & Tips

The longer you leave this the better it will get and the more flavour into the meat

Don't throw away the marinade left over, use it in your dish to add more flavour

Please wash and re-use the bag when finished!

## Lemon & Peppercorn

### Ingredients

- 1 lemon zested and juiced
- 1 tbspn black peppercorns
- 2 tbspns rapeseed or olive oil

### Method

Put all ingredients into the bag

Add the meat of your choice as you will be cooking it, ie strips, chunks, whole

Close the bag getting as much of the air out before you zip it up

Gently massage the mix together and around the meat so it is completely covered

KEY Leave for a minimum of an hour but preferably in the fridge overnight

When you are ready to cook, take the meat out of the bag and remove any excess marinade

Cook as you wish!

## Ginger & Lemongrass

### Ingredients

- 2 tspns chopped ginger
- 1 lemongrass stick
- 2 tbspns rapeseed or olive oil

### Method

Bash the lemongrass stick with a rolling pin or something heave just to squash it to release the flavours

Put all ingredients into the bag

Add the meat of your choice as you will be cooking it, ie strips, chunks, whole

Close the bag getting as much of the air out before you zip it up

Gently massage the mix together and around the meat so it is completely covered

KEY Leave for a minimum of an hour but preferably in the fridge overnight

When you are ready to cook, take the meat out of the bag and remove any excess marinade

Cook as you wish!

### Hints & Tips

The longer you leave this the better it will get and the more flavour into the meat

Don't throw away the marinade left over, use it in your dish to add more flavour

Please wash and re-use the bag when finished!

## Chilli, Coriander & Lime

### Ingredients

- 1 bunch fresh coriander
- 2 tspns dried chilli flakes
- 1 lime zested and juiced
- 2 Tbspns rapeseed or olive oil

### Method

Put all ingredients into the bag

Add the meat of your choice as you will be cooking it, ie strips, chunks, whole

Close the bag getting as much of the air out before you zip it up

Gently massage the mix together and around the meat so it is completely covered

KEY Leave for a minimum of an hour but preferably in the fridge overnight

When you are ready to cook, take the meat out of the bag and remove any excess marinade

Cook as you wish!

## BBQ

### Ingredients

1 tspn smoked paprika

1 tspn dried chilli flakes

1 lime zested and juiced

1 tspn chopped garlic

Small bunch of fresh coriander

2 tbspns rapeseed or olive oil

### Method

Put all ingredients into the bag

Add the meat of your choice as you will be cooking it, ie strips, chunks, whole

Close the bag getting as much of the air out before you zip it up

Gently massage the mix together and around the meat so it is completely covered

KEY Leave for a minimum of an hour but preferably in the fridge overnight

When you are ready to cook, take the meat out of the bag and remove any excess marinade

Cook as you wish!

### Hints & Tips

The longer you leave this the better it will get and the more flavour into the meat

Don't throw away the marinade left over, use it in your dish to add more flavour

Please wash and re-use the bag when finished!

## Honey & Soy

### Ingredients

- 1 tbspns honey
- 1 tbspn gluten free soy sauce
- 2 tbspns rapeseed or olive oil

### Method

Put all ingredients into the bag

Add the meat of your choice as you will be cooking it, ie strips, chunks, whole

Close the bag getting as much of the air out before you zip it up

Gently massage the mix together and around the meat so it is completely covered

KEY Leave for a minimum of an hour but preferably in the fridge overnight

When you are ready to cook, take the meat out of the bag and remove any excess marinade

Cook as you wish!

### Hints & Tips

The longer you leave this the better it will get and the more flavour into the meat

Don't throw away the marinade left over, use it in your dish to add more flavour

Please wash and re-use the bag when finished!

## Honey, Orange & Ginger

### Ingredients

- 2 tbspns honey
- 1 tspn chopped ginger
- 1 tspn chopped garlic
- 2 tbspns gluten free soy sauce
- ½ orange zested and juiced
- 2 tbspns orange marmalade
- 2 tbspns rapeseed or olive oil

### Method

Put all ingredients into the bag

Add the meat of your choice as you will be cooking it, ie strips, chunks, whole

Close the bag getting as much of the air out before you zip it up

Gently massage the mix together and around the meat so it is completely covered

KEY Leave for a minimum of an hour but preferably in the fridge overnight

When you are ready to cook, take the meat out of the bag and remove any excess marinade

Cook as you wish!

### Hints & Tips

The longer you leave this the better it will get and the more flavour into the meat

Don't throw away the marinade left over, use it in your dish to add more flavour

Please wash and re-use the bag when finished!

# Dried Herb Mix For Pastas

*Great to have made up – for anything!*

**Difficult rating:** ★☆☆☆☆
**Serves:** as many as you use
**Cooking time:** 0 mins
**Preparation time:** 10 mins
**Give Yourself Time:** 15 mins

## You Will Need

*Small bowl*
*Teaspoon*
*Small jar or bottle to store that has an airtight lid*

## Ingredients

- 1 tspn garlic granules (dried not fresh)
- 1 tspn salt
- 1 tspn dried chilli flakes
- 1 tspn dried parsley
- 1 tspn dried basil

## Method

Add all the ingredients to the bowl

Mix well with a spoon or your fingers

Use and/or store!

## Hints & Tips

Make it up in the vessel you will be using to store it in – makes life easier

Have a great smell of this as it is wonderful!

Add to any pasta dish, plain pasta through to a full bake

It also works on white meat and fish

## Ways To Change

Add some smoked garlic granules rather than plain

Same with some smoked salt

# Salt!

*Bear with me!*

**Difficult rating:** ★☆☆☆☆
**Cooking time:** 0 mins
**Preparation time:** 5 mins
**Give Yourself Time:** 10 mins

**You Will Need**

*Knife*
*Chopping board*
*Plate*
*Teaspoon*

Salt can have a bad name, and rightly so if you use it too much, so moderate it and use it wisely

In salads, a pinch of sea salt crystals can make a massive difference and bring our natural flavours.

Just try some of the following and taste the difference!

Have them as they are or as part of a built up salad,

## Beef Tomatoes

**Ingredients**

- 2-3 beef tomatoes thinly sliced into rounds
- Sea salt crystals

**Method**

Arrange the slices of tomato thinly on a plate

Sprinkle sea salt over them all and just wait...

Tastes amazing!

## Radishes

**Ingredients**

- 10 – 15 radishes sliced thinly into rounds
- Sea salt crystals

**Method**

Arrange the slices of radish thinly on a plate

Sprinkle sea salt over them all and just wait...

Tastes amazing!

## Onion

**Ingredients**

- 1 large white or red or ½ each mixed onion, peeled and sliced into rounds
- Sea salt crystals

**Method**

Arrange the slices of onion thinly on a plate

Sprinkle sea salt over them all and just wait...

Tastes amazing!

## Avocado

**Ingredients**

- 2 ripe avocados, cut in half
- Sea salt crystals

**Method**

Remove the stone from one half of the avocadoes, and carefully remove the flesh with a teaspoon run around the inside of the skin

Slice the avocados into half-moon shapes

Arrange the slices of avocado thinly on a plate

Sprinkle sea salt over them all and just wait...

Tastes amazing!

# Salad Dressings

*Home-made is best!*

**Difficult rating:** ★☆☆☆☆
**Cooking time:** 0 mins
**Preparation time:** 10 mins
**Give Yourself Time:** 15 mins

**You Will Need**

*Teaspoon*
*Knife*
*Chopping board*
*Tablespoon*
*Small bowl*

Use your new found infused oil skills *(see recipes on pages 132-132)* and already you have a great dressing! Here are a couple more very simple and quick ones to try

## Lemon & Herb

**Ingredients**

- 1 lemon juiced
- 1 tspn Italian mixed herbs
- 4 tbsns extra virgin olive oil (use your lemon oil if you have any made)

**Method**

Add all of the ingredients to the bowl

Mix well to combine. Serve!

## Crème Freche & Mustard

**Ingredients**

- 1 tbspn crème freche
- 1 tspn grainy mustard
- 4 tablespoons extra virgin olive oil

**Method**

Add all of the ingredients to the bowl

Mix well to combine. Serve!

## Greek Yoghurt & Citrus

**Ingredients**

- 2 tbspns plain Greek yoghurt
- 2 tbspns extra virgin olive oil
- ½ orange juiced
- ½ lime or ½ lemon juiced

**Method**

Add all of the ingredients to the bowl

Mix well to combine. Serve!

## Soy & Balsamic

**Ingredients**

- 3 tbspns extra virgin olive oil
- 1 tbspn balsamic vinegar
- 1 tspn dash gluten free soy sauce

**Method**

Add all of the ingredients to the bowl

Mix well to combine. Serve!

## Honey & Mustard

**Ingredients**

- 2 tspns wholegrain mustard
- 2 tspns honey
- 1 lemon juiced
- 6 tbspns extra virgin olive oil

**Method**

Add all of the ingredients to the bowl

Mix well to combine. Serve!

**Hints & Tips**

You can keep these in the fridge in airtight containers for a good week

Double up the amounts to make more

# Groundhog Day

You've probably seen the film
Where Bill Murray fulfils the same day
Until he realises that to get the girl
He needs to act a different way

Chronic pain in a household
Can seem the exact same way
In a non-escapable spiral
There just doesn't seem any new day

The world becomes focussed on days at a time
Hours, minutes, no seconds
It literally becomes a battle to survive
Thank heck we don't own any weapons

One person only can accept these days
The same thing over and over again
Sleeping a lot, watching TV
Wallowing in self-pity and pain

The other is having to do everything
Their own job and that of the other
A single parent now massively overloaded
Wondering why the hell should they bother

The swear words are muttered under their breath
I just wish he'd try and do anything
But oblivious to the plight of their embattled partner
The pain is a pain in the .......... something

So how do you break the Groundhog Day cycle
It takes joint effort, communication and luck
It's really hard work but it can be done
I'm living proof now writing this book

It comes back to values and what do you want
Is the life you are leading so fair
To get back as a father, a husband, a man
All you need to do is care!

www.ingramcontent.com/pod-product-compliance
Lightning Source LLC
LaVergne TN
LVHW060623110826
845147LV00015B/923